BT 6 08

THE COMPLETE GUIDE TO INVESTING IN COMMODITY TRADING AND FUTURES

HOW TO EARN HIGH RATES OF RETURNS SAFELY

BY MARY B. HOLIHAN

THE COMPLETE GUIDE TO INVESTING IN COMMODITY TRADING & FUTURES: HOW TO EARN HIGH RATES OF RETURNS SAFELY

Copyright © 2008 by Atlantic Publishing Group, Inc.
1405 SW 6th Ave. • Ocala, Florida 34471 • 800-814-1132 • 352-622-1875–Fax
Web site: www.atlantic-pub.com • E-mail: sales@atlantic-pub.com
SAN Number: 268-1250

ISBN-13: 978-1-60138-003-6   ISBN-10: 1-60138-003-8

Library of Congress Cataloging-in-Publication Data

Holihan, Mary B., 1947-
  The complete guide to investing in commodity trading & futures : how to earn high rates of returns safely / by Mary B. Holihan.
       p. cm.
  Includes bibliographical references and index.
  ISBN-13: 978-1-60138-003-6 (alk. paper)
  ISBN-10: 1-60138-003-8 (alk. paper)
  1. Commodity exchanges--United States--Handbooks, manuals, etc. 2. Futures market--United States--Handbooks, manuals, etc. I. Title.

  HG6049.H65 2008
  332.64'4--dc22
                         2008011366

INTERIOR LAYOUT DESIGN: Vickie Taylor • vtaylor@atlantic-pub.com

Printed in the United States

Printed on Recycled Paper

We recently lost our beloved pet "Bear," who was not only our best and dearest friend but also the "Vice President of Sunshine" here at Atlantic Publishing. He did not receive a salary but worked tirelessly 24 hours a day to please his parents. Bear was a rescue dog that turned around and showered myself, my wife Sherri, his grandparents Jean, Bob and Nancy and every person and animal he met (maybe not rabbits) with friendship and love. He made a lot of people smile every day.

We wanted you to know that a portion of the profits of this book will be donated to The Humane Society of the United States.

–Douglas & Sherri Brown

THE HUMANE SOCIETY
OF THE UNITED STATES©

The human-animal bond is as old as human history. We cherish our animal companions for their unconditional affection and acceptance. We feel a thrill when we glimpse wild creatures in their natural habitat or in our own backyard.

Unfortunately, the human-animal bond has at times been weakened. Humans have exploited some animal species to the point of extinction.

The Humane Society of the United States makes a difference in the lives of animals here at home and worldwide. The HSUS is dedicated to creating a world where our relationship with animals is guided by compassion. We seek a truly humane society in which animals are respected for their intrinsic value, and where the human-animal bond is strong.

Want to help animals? We have plenty of suggestions. Adopt a pet from a local shelter, join The Humane Society and be a part of our work to help companion animals and wildlife. You will be funding our educational, legislative, investigative and outreach projects in the U.S. and across the globe.

Or perhaps you'd like to make a memorial donation in honor of a pet, friend or relative? You can through our Kindred Spirits program. And if you'd like to contribute in a more structured way, our Planned Giving Office has suggestions about estate planning, annuities, and even gifts of stock that avoid capital gains taxes.

Maybe you have land that you would like to preserve as a lasting habitat for wildlife. Our Wildlife Land Trust can help you. Perhaps the land you want to share is a backyard—that's enough. Our Urban Wildlife Sanctuary Program will show you how to create a habitat for your wild neighbors.

So you see, it's easy to help animals. And The HSUS is here to help.

The Humane Society of the United States
2100 L Street NW
Washington, DC 20037
202-452-1100
www.hsus.org

DEDICATION

I am deeply grateful to my wonderful family and friends and to the love of my life, Kevin, for constant, unwavering support.

TABLE OF CONTENTS

INTRODUCTION

A lot of people make a lot of money in commodities. A lot of people lose a lot of money in commodities. The days of buying a real estate property for $5,000 and turning it around to a profit of $100,000 are long over, but in the commodities futures markets, it is still possible to turn $5,000 into hundreds of thousands. For example, Richard Dennis, the "Prince of the Pit", started in the Chicago Board of Trade as a "runner" and over a ten-year period parlayed a few thousand dollar investment into a fortune of more than $200 million. Dennis' firm belief was that successful trading was a talent that could be learned and it was not an innate talent, possessed by only a few gifted individuals.

The efficiency of markets, combined with the seemingly unlimited information capacity of the internet has made information regarding markets, commodities, trading systems, news, etc. quickly available to any market participant who seeks them out. In this book, you will see how using the vast amount of information available to everyone can be used to become a successful trader. The problem for most people is they insist on treating commodities trading as a get-rich quick scheme, akin to playing the lottery or gambling in a casino. Commodity trading is a business; just as in any business, you do the proper research, build a plan, and examine your risks before you make each sale, deal, or transaction. This is what separates the professionals from the amateurs. As in any business, hard work and dedication yields results; profits don't just "happen." The people who lose big are the ones who do not have the patience to study the available information, are not willing to wait out markets, perhaps most importantly, are not able to control their risks but instead take big risks in the hopes of winning big in a very short time. Take the example of Richard Dennis above. Two hundred million dollars is certainly a great fortune, but he studied and worked the markets for ten years to achieve this impressive result.

As you decide whether to enter the speculative commodities trading market, the first step is to be aware of all of the risks involved, analyze them, and, above all, be comfortable with them. In any area of business (or even life!), risk cannot be eliminated, but it can be managed. For the most part, through the use of stop-loss orders, hedging, and staying informed about the market, losses can be predicted and managed. In the event of major market moves, the losses can mount up, but even those can be restricted by an important guidelines we will discuss in this book, including one of the most important ones, "never answer a margin call". Using conservative trading methods such as the one you will learn here allows a trader to control losses within reasonable limits, determined by the risk he can afford to take. Traders who cannot face the inevitability of loss should not be trading at all; most successful traders look at their losses as a cost of doing business, cut or minimize them as quickly as possible, learn from them, and then move on to the next trade.

PART ONE

THE BASICS

COMMODITY BASICS

"Chance favors the informed mind."
— Louis Pasteur

THE CONCEPT OF COMMODITIES

Commodities are the basic raw materials of just about everything we eat and use. As such, they have been sold and traded for thousands of years as man discovered a use for each kind of commodity. Most of the products traded in the commodity markets are essential to life as we know it: food products, metals and oil. We survive on food, build our economies with metals, and power them with oil. Unsurprisingly, agricultural commodities were the first commodities to be traded in a "futures" market; the concept is eons old, as we shall observe, and has spread to many other raw materials and has now grown to include that rawest material of all, money. In addition to agricultural commodities, metals (such as gold and silver), and oil and petroleum-based products, there are futures contracts for "intangible" commodities such as interest rates, currencies, and bond and stock market indices. (The commodity is the actual good that is traded; commodity futures are exchanged on commodity exchanges. Commodity futures are also called derivatives. There are many types of derivatives trading because the value of the future is derived from the actual good.)

How did the first commodities futures markets come to be formed? It all started, as we would expect, with the human survival need for foodstuffs. Maintaining a year-round supply of seasonal crops and products has always been problematic, and solving this problem led to a system that we know today as the futures trading markets. The first recorded instance of futures trading occurred in the rice trade in 17th century Japan, although there is also evidence indicating rice futures in China 6,000 years ago. In the precursor to today's futures trading system, these 17th century Japanese merchants would store rice in warehouses for future use. To raise cash while they held these stocks of rice, the warehouse owners sold receipts against the stored rice, known as "rice tickets." Over time, these rice tickets became accepted as a kind of general commercial currency, especially since rice was such a pervasive commodity of the entire economy. To assure that everyone could understand the value of the rice tickets, and to make sure there were common standards to indicate the value of each ticket, rules were gradually developed that standardized the trading of these rice tickets. Eventually, futures trading as we know it today grew out of these rules. We will see how the principle of "rice tickets" is mimicked in the concept of original warehouse receipts that made modern commodities futures trading possible.

Commodity markets, in one form or another, have persevered. Even during medieval times, when culture was destroyed or ignored and society became relatively static, trade associations organized by merchants continued the tradition of "bringing things to market." An interesting study by Gregory Clark of the department of economics at University of California-Davis, Markets and Economic Growth: The Grain Market of Medieval England showed how these ancient traders were able to bring efficiency to markets that is still today the hallmark of commodities trading. For example, in a very thorough analysis of the prices of grain in the various manors of southeast England during the years 1300-1349, he showed that if prices were lower on some manors than others because they had grain surpluses, the price gap represented the transportation costs of the consumers of the grain in the distant areas. This "efficient market" hypothesis still rules grain prices today. Distances between producing and consuming areas explain price differentials because transfer costs, which today, of course, include loading or handling the grain and transportation charges, which include equipment and fuel prices are the most important variables in determining grain price differentials. For this reason, price differentials between regions cannot exceed transfer costs for very long. If this situation occurs, equilibrium will quickly be found as buyers purchase commodities from the low-priced market (raising prices there) and ship them to the higher-priced market (lowering prices there). As we have seen, this market pricing mechanism has existed for hundreds of years.

So we can see that these ancient markets are the precursor of the exchanges that we have today. But the real foundation of the commodity exchanges that trade many of the products discussed in this book has its roots in the Chicago Board of Trade, in the mid-1800s.

As is the case with so many of the advances of the 19th century industrial revolution, the invention of the steam locomotive was the engine (pun aside) of growth for the commodities markets. The railroad made high volumes of grain shipment possible and allowed farmers to secure larger loans on their crops. These loans traditionally were secured by warehouse receipts (following the tradition of the Japanese rice tickets of two hundred years prior) for a particular quantity of grain. This increased volume led to active transfer and trading of these warehouse receipts. This required that grains be "fungible," or according to Merriam-Webster's dictionary, "being of such a nature that one part or quantity may be replaced by another equal part or quantity in the satisfaction of an obligation." Commodities, options, and securities are all considered fungible assets since they can be freely interchanged. For example, an investor's shares of IBM held for the investor by a brokerage firm are freely mixed with other customers' IBM shares. By the same token, stock options are interchangeable among investors, and a quantity of wheat stored in a grain elevator is not specifically identified as to its ownership. In this manner, grain warehouse receipts could be used as an exchangeable representation of the underlying good in order to act as collateral for a loan.

These loans could be more easily secured if the underlying collateral had a firm price and quantity commitments from a buyer. This is why merchants began to engage in forward contracts. According to Thomas Hieronymus, in his book

Economics of Futures Trading for Commercial and Personal Profit, the first such "time contract" on record was made on March 13, 1851. It specified that 3,000 bushels of corn were to be delivered to Chicago in June at a price of one cent below the March 13 cash market price. Still today, this is almost exactly the way a futures contact would be quoted on a futures exchange.

HOW THE COMMODITY MARKET FUNCTIONS

All futures markets function in the same way: they are markets in which commodities or financial instruments are bought and sold for purchase or delivery at some future date. Each of these agreements to buy or sell is called a futures contract. When futures are traded, nothing is actually bought or sold, just the right to a contract representing a given quantity of a good. Traders buy and sell these futures contracts with the expectation of either selling them at a higher price or buying them back at a lower price, thereby earning a profit, with no actual interest in the corn or whatever commodity the contract represents. Before the expiration period of the contract is over, the buyer or seller will offset his position. That is, he will sell enough contracts to zero out his purchases of contracts, or he will buy enough contracts to zero out his sales of contracts. If he guessed right on the direction of the price movement, he will sell the contracts for more than he paid for them or he will buy the contracts at a lower price than he sold them for and he will make a profit; if he guessed wrong, he will have to sell the contracts for less than he paid or buy the contracts for more than he sold and he will incur a loss.

Each futures contract traded is for a very specific quantity of a very specific commodity. In other words, when a trader offers to buy a contract of soybeans, he knows he is dealing with a promise to buy 5,000 bushels of "GMO or a mixture of GMO and Non-GMO No. 2 yellow soybeans of Indiana, Ohio and Michigan origin produced in the U.S.A. (Non-screened, stored in silo)," and of deliverable grade if they are "GMO or a mixture of GMO and Non-GMO No. 2 yellow soybeans of Iowa, Illinois and Wisconsin origin produced in the U.S.A. The buyer of this soybean contract does not necessarily care that the beans are from Indiana or Ohio, but only that it is a exact grade that will match the grade that he will have to sell when he liquidates the position to make his profit. Each commodity is traded on its own exchange and has its own such standard. Thus, a coffee contract on the New York Coffee Exchange is for 37,500 pounds of one of the five grades of coffee traded on that exchange, a corn contract on the Chicago Board of Trade is for 5,000 bushels of corn, and a British Pound contract on the Comex is for £62,500. The exchanges require that all contracts represent a standard grade of the product. Gasoline futures traded on the NYMEX are based on the contract specifications for "New York Harbor Unleaded Gasoline." In this way, everyone is comparing apples to apples. Finally, there is standardization in each contract's minimum price fluctuation, or "tick," based on the underlying measurement of the commodity. Therefore, the price fluctuation for coffee is 10 cents per ounce, for corn, ¼ cents per bushel, etc. Except for grains, minimum fluctuations are generally quoted in points.

These are basically four legs of a commodity contract: how much of a given quantity of a commodity is being traded, what the exact specification of the commodity is, the delivery date, and the payment specifications. Some contracts may also have daily price limits; this is the maximum amount that the market can move above or below the previous day's close in a trading session. Exchanges decide whether a commodity has a trading limit and how much it is. The Exchanges use this limit move rule to slow markets down when dramatic price swings occur. A commodity can trade up to or down to the limit price, but not above or below it. If there are too many buyers chasing too few sellers, the market locks at the limit up price, and if there are too many sellers and not enough buyers, the market locks at the limit down price.

The theory behind this "limit-move" rule is to allow markets to cool down when there are violent price moves. The soybean contract on the CBOT, for example is only allowed to move up or down 50¢ per bushel from the previous day's close. If the market closed at $8.00 on Monday, then on Tuesday it would only be allowed to trade as high at $8.50 or as low as $7.50; the price offered cannot go above $8.50 or below $7.50. In volatile markets, the price can move to the limit and then, since it can go no further, it will "lock" at that price. Lock limit up means that there are too many buyers versus sellers at the limit price and lock limit down means that there are too many sellers versus buyers at the limit price.

The other important element of the commodity futures market is the concept of clearing. Each buyer or seller does not really exchange a contract for an amount of money. This is next to impossible because off-setting purchases and sales between traders rarely balance with respect to quantity. A brokerage firm will do business with a clearinghouse, the ultimate buyer and seller of commodity contracts. Simply put, the clearinghouse matches buyers with sellers, and this is one of the most important components of commodities trading.

Each of the futures exchanges has its own clearing house and all members of the exchange are required to clear their trades through their clearing house at the end of each trading session. (They are also required to deposit with the clearing house a sum of money based on clearinghouse margin requirements sufficient to cover the member's debit balance, but we will discuss margin requirements in detail later on.) For example, a member broker reports to the clearing house at the end of the day total purchase of 100,000 bushels of July corn and total sales of 50,000 bushels of July corn, he would be long 50,000 bushels of July corn. On the clearing house side, there has to be some customer, or total of customers that are short 50,000 bushels of July corn, since for every purchase of a contract, there has to be an offsetting sale of the same contract.

Trading in frenzied markets have been suspended when there is an imbalance between buy and sell orders to allow the clearinghouse to catch up on these matches and make sure no one can back out of a contract that is no longer attractive. This kind of frenzied buying or selling is usually fueled by speculation and the suspension of trading allows the market to cool, as well as allowing the trades to balance properly.

WHERE ARE COMMODITIES TRADED?

Today there are ten commodities exchanges in the United States, the largest of which are the Chicago Board of Trade, the Chicago Mercantile Exchange, the New York Mercantile Exchange, the New York Commodity Exchange and the New York Coffee, Sugar and Cocoa Exchange. Of these large exchanges, NYMEX is the only one that trades only commodities, and therefore is the world's largest commodity exchange. There are also exchanges in more than 20 countries worldwide and the commodities traded on them typically reflect the commercial or agricultural specialty of the area. For example, barely and oats are traded on the Winnipeg Commodity Exchange, in the center of the area where these products are grown. Of the thirty major Exchanges throughout the world, 80% of the world's business is conducted on the most active dozen. Each of the major commodity exchanges specializes in certain areas. The Chicago Board of Trade is the home to grain and treasury futures and is the oldest U.S. exchange. The Chicago Mercantile Exchange is the largest exchange in the world; livestock, currencies, and stock index futures are traded on "the Merc." The Coffee, Sugar and Cocoa Exchange trades the commodities that are listed in its name. The New York Cotton Exchange is home to cotton and orange juice futures. Crude oil contracts are traded through the New York Mercantile Exchange, and the Comex Division of the New York Mercantile Exchange is where gold and other metals futures are traded. And, as we shall see later, some exchanges have been formed and then died out due to lack of participation.

There are three major commodity exchanges in the United Kingdom-the London International Financial Futures Exchange (LIFFE), the London Metals Exchange and the Intercontinental Exchange (ICE-formerly the International Petroleum Exchange). LIFFE is the biggest futures exchange in Europe, specializing in futures contracts on financial instruments such as the Eurodollar and the Eurobund, as well as cocoa, sugar, coffee, wheat, barley, potatoes and other agricultural products. The London Metals Exchange offers futures and options contracts for aluminum, copper, nickel, tin, zinc and lead, and in 2005, it launched the first futures contract for plastics: polypropylene and linear low density polyethylene. Crude oil, gas, oil, natural gas, electricity coal and ECX carbon financial instruments are traded on the ICE Futures Europe.

Japan also has a major exchange, the Central Japan Commodity Exchange based in Nagoya, Japan. It was formed in 1996 from the merger of three other major exchanges and trades commodities ranging from eggs to gasoline and kerosene to ferrous scrap.

Until 1993, the exchanges in the United States accounted for the major part of the futures and options trading in the world. This is no longer the case as other exchanges have become more active and in total, trade more than is traded on the U.S. exchanges. There are a number of large futures exchanges in Argentina and Brazil, notably the Bolsa de Mercadorias & Futuros of Brazil. There are many exchanges which primarily trade in physical commodities for immediate or forward deliver in El Salvador, Hondoras, Nicuaragua, Costa Rica, Panama, Colombia, Ecuador and

Peru which have been created in response to liberalization of trade and as a mechanism for local commodity trade flows. (UNCTAD-Commodity Exchanges Around the World, 1999).

In other words, there are futures exchanges in every region of the world, from Bulgaria to South Africa to Indonesia, but the exchanges in the United States and the United Kingdom predominate the volume of trade.

HOW ARE COMMODITY FUTURES TRADED?

Now that we know that the futures contract is a basic unit of exchange on the futures markets, we have to understand just how they are traded. A futures contract is a legally binding agreement to deliver the given quantity at a fixed date in the future. In reality, very few traders ever "take delivery" of the contracts they are trading. In fact, less than 2% of all futures contracts have a delivery associated with them. What simply happens is that the difference in price is settled between buyers and sellers. This is called offset, and with an offset, the trader makes the opposite trade (he buys if he has sold or sells if he has bought) for the same delivery period, to zero out the position he was holding. Because of the concepts of fungibility and standardization discussed above and the operations of the commodity exchanges, this all happens very easily.

Using the basics we have just covered, let us look at an actual trade. Trader Joe believes that the price of corn will continue to rise because of the increasing demand for ethanol (made from corn), and the charts indicate a strong trend for prices to continue upward (more about charts and trends later). Trader Joe also could have traded in ethanol itself if he wanted to. He decides to buy corn contracts to hold onto for a while for a profit. On Monday, he buys 100 contracts of December delivery corn (representing 500,000 bushels) at $3.645 per bushel. Corn futures end higher on Tuesday, boosted by speculative buying after Monday's crop progress report revealed lower than expected corn plantings. (This is simple economic concept of supply and demand; if there is less corn planted, there will be means lower quantities yielded, which will lead to higher prices.) This is not the reason he had bought the corn, but he decides to take his profit and reenter the market at a later date, perhaps after the market has settled down and absorbed the reduced plantings news. Each delivery period for corn is affected by news of the expected corn plantings, so May corn gained 9.50 cents to $3.6750 per bushel, July settled 10 cents higher at $3.7750, and our friend's December corn rallied 14 cents to $3.7850! Because of the efficiency of the clearing system, he can sell his 100 contracts for a profit of $70,000. Of course, the opposite could have happened and the price could have fallen 14 cents, but let us assume that in this case, our savvy trader, who is following a long-term trend, would have just held onto his position. He was just taking temporary advantage of this "uptick" in the price.

If you are bearish on a commodity (in other words, you expect the price to go down), you can do the exact opposite. Trader Dan, who thinks all this hype about ethanol is overplayed and is interpreting the charts to read some resistance levels, thinks the price of corn is poised to fall, so he decides to sell December corn. He sells 100 contracts at $3.645. (For the sake of this argument, we will use the same price and ignore the bid/offer spread; we've also left out the concept of commissions and transaction costs.) The news of the crop progress report is not good news for him, and now he wonders whether he should be paying more attention to the other fundamentals, such as plantings, weather, crop yields, etc. If he had the courage of his convictions, he may stick with his short position until the price comes down and he can buy it back at his target price of $3.545. If the crop progress report had shown higher than average plantings, and the price met resistance as he suspected it would, this could easily have happened, and he would have made $50,000 on his short sale. If he sells now because he thinks he may have been wrong about the market direction, he will lose $70,000. Should he sell or hold his position?

This is the kind of situation commodity traders face every day.

MARGIN AND LEVERAGE

Adding to the uncertainty is the concept of margin and leverage. Leverage is the ability to buy futures contracts on "margin." This means that you can trade futures by putting up a certain percentage of the value of the future contracts. This minimum amount must be maintained in the client's account. The margin deposit required is set by the Exchange on which the commodity is traded and ranges from as little as 2% to 10%. In addition, the broker may have his own additional margin requirements.

Here's how it works: Let us say that in order to trade corn futures on the Chicago Board of Trade you have to deposit an initial margin requirement of $450 per contract. (The exchanges adjust the margins based on the amount of volatility in the market. In a volatile market, the exchange raises the initial margins to make sure that positions can still be covered in a quickly moving market.) This will secure the trade of 5,000 bushels of corn, since one contract of corn is for 5,000 bushels. If we use the prices in our Trader Joe and Trader Dan examples above, this means that for $450, a trader could control $18,925 worth of corn futures with his $450 margin deposit. (The math: 5,000 bushels x $3.7850.) Margin is a double-edged sword, however. Yes, one contract of corn can be bought for $3.645 and sold for $3.785, yielding a $700 profit on a $450 deposit (and note that it is a deposit, not an investment — when the $700 is realized, it is added to the $450 margin deposit in the account). But if the price of corn went DOWN 14 cents, the trader would have lost the $450 margin and still owed $350 to cover the loss. Multiply these results by thousands of contracts, and it is easy to see how the concept of leverage and margins can make for very exciting and risky trading.

HOW COMMODITY FUTURES COMPARES TO OTHER INVESTMENTS

Commodity futures are still a relatively unexploited asset class in terms of the average investor's portfolio, despite being traded for hundreds of years. Commodity futures are very different than the stocks and bonds found in most private portfolios. The most notable differences are that they are what is considered "derivative securities," in other words, they do not represent a claim on a given corporation or government, as a stock or bond does, but only on a contract that represents a good. Commodities are also claims on assets, as stocks and bonds are, but only short term claims, whereas stocks and bonds represent long term claims on the company. A final difference is that commodities have a marked seasonality that results in a great deal of volatility in prices; an investment in the ownership (equity) of a company or in its debt (bonds) may have some basic cyclical pressures, based on the type of business, but not the day to day volatility seen in commodities.

Another, and perhaps the most important reason that commodity futures are relatively unknown may be more commonplace, namely, data is not reported in as widespread a manner. Unlike the data on the stock market, which is today a standard part of the evening news, and mentioned frequently on TV and radio news, reporting on commodity futures is limited to a ticker band on the bottom of cable news channels, or perhaps a quick summary on stations dedicated to the financial news. Of course, this is also a function of the popularity of stocks over commodities as investment vehicles. There is a lot of data available covering every commodity, but the investor has to seek it out. (An exception might be when a commodity has a major impact on the everyday life of the consumer. During escalating gas and oil prices, the general press actively reports the per barrel price of crude oil on a daily basis.)

Another reason that commodities are not part of the everyman portfolio may be that the entire function of corporate securities such as stocks and bonds is very different from that of commodities. Stocks and bonds represent the liabilities of firms, and are used to raise money for the company. Investors risk that future profits of the company may deteriorate or even disappear in bad times such as recessions or slowdowns in a given industry. Claims on the equity of a company represent the current value of future cash flows over the long term. Investors are compensated for the risks they take by owning a part of the company and bestowing confidence upon the management team of the company. The investor is to a great extent an integral part of the company, as both an owner who has put his capital at risk and as an assessor of the performance of the company's management.

This is where investing in a company through its stocks and bonds and trading in commodity futures differ greatly. Commodity futures do not raise any funds for a company, and they do not represent ownership in or credit to a company. The purpose of commodity futures is allow firms involved in the underlying commodity to obtain insure against unexpected fluctuations in the price of theses commodities, either as an income or as an expense, depending on whether the company is a producer or a consumer. Farmers who want to depend on a given price for their crops and food processors who want to count on a given price for their ingredients will sell or buy the relevant commodity in the futures market to give them this assurance, and they count on speculators to act as counter parties in these transactions. Investors in commodity futures receive compensation for bearing the risk of short-term commodity price fluctuations that the farmer or the processor does not want to bear. This kind of activity may seem too much like gambling to the average investor.

We discussed the fact that if you buy contracts in corn futures, you would not have to worry about the delivery of all of that corn-buying commodity futures does not mean a direct exposure to the actual commodity. This is where a sense of gambling does come into play since traders are gambling on the future spot price of the commodity. The level of supply of a commodity at current and future dates links the spot price and the expected future spot price. There are many differences, however, between the various commodities, and hence how the futures of a given commodity will behave. Some commodities store easily and for long periods of time (oil and gas, platinum and gold, for instance). Others are more or less perishable or have limited life spans (grains, orange juice, livestock). Some are basic raw materials that require further processing or refining (crude oil, soybeans) than others (gold, feedcorn). These factors will all influence how the futures price of the commodity will behave.

COMMODITY PITS AND KEY PLAYERS

Another important aspect of commodity trading is the physical function of the trade. Trades take place in the commodity "pits." If you have ever seen a commodities exchange, either in person or on TV, you have seen frantic people waving their hands and yelling. Even though it may look like chaos, there is a system in place that actually renders the trading process quite organized, as we shall see later. There are a number of personalities who are the key players in the commodity markets, and who make this organization work because they understand and play their roles so well.

Hedgers

First of all, there are hedgers, who are different from speculators. These would consist of the farmers and processors we used in the above example and the thousands of others like them in various industries, either producing or using raw materials. They are outright hedgers. They are also known as the commercials. Hedgers deal in the commodity at hand and are seeking to protect themselves against adverse price movements. They rely on speculators to offer them this price protection.

Speculators

Speculators are there to profit from the price swings. Speculators are traders who have no intention of producing or processing the commodities they buy or sell. Their only intention is to make money. Typically, they use the concept of leveraging to make large sums of money on small price movements in the markets. These speculative operators in the pits are often referred to as the "locals." Locals are traders who make trades for their own account. There are a number of different ways in which these speculators trade.

Day traders

One type of speculator that is often spoken of is the "day trader," who takes a position in futures and then liquidates it before the end of the day. Day traders buy and sell commodities all through the day in the hope that the commodity they have bought or sold will continue to increase or fall in value during the few moments that they are holding the position, yielding them a profit. A day trader will monitor commodities on his computer screen in the hope of identifying those that are continuing a trend up or down in value, even for just a short while. They will try to ride this momentum and liquidate the position and take their profit before the price direction changes. Momentum is the most important factor for a day trader; they just want to ride an upswing or downswing long enough to profit from this momentum. A day trader typically will not hold a commodity position overnight because this momentum may not hold from one day to the next. Daytrading is a very stressful job since the trader cannot leave his computer for a moment for fear the momentum will run out when he is not looking. It also takes a lot of stamina and concentration to watch multiple commodities to spot the ones that are beginning a short term trend. In addition, because they are constantly buying and selling their positions, they are subject to high commission expenses.

Scalpers

A "scalper" is a trader who trades for small gains: He may establish a position and then buy or sell out of it within minutes or hours. Scalping is a method of arbitraging small price gaps created by the bid/ask spread. Markets such as equity trading, foreign exchange and commodities all operate on a bid and ask based system. The difference between the bid and the ask prices is the spread. To "make the spread" means to buy at the bid price and sell at the ask price. They can make a profit as long as there are traders in the market who are willing to pay the market price. The ask price is the price for immediate execution of a trade, at market, for a buyer who wants to close the trade quickly; the bid price is the price for immediate execution for a seller who wants to close the trade quickly. When trades are executed at market prices, the trader would automatically lose that spread if he closed out that trade immediately. A scalper will wait for his contract to be executed in order to receive the spread premium. Which traders will execute at market prices despite the bid/ask spread, allowing the scalpers to operate? Traders who need to move quickly, such as day traders who are trading on momentum, need to get into a position as quickly as possible to take advantage of the momentum, and also need to get out as soon as they can when the momentum direction changes. Traders who are looking to cut losses and get out of a position quickly will also pay the bid/offer spread. Scalping is another type of trading that involves buying or selling positions quickly, sometimes within seconds of establishing them.

Spreaders

A "spreader" is a trader who buys and sells two related markets expecting a profit when the positions are offset. There are different types of spreads. For example, buying a contract of corn for one month and selling a contract of corn for a different delivery month (intramarket spread); buying and selling the same contact for the same delivery month, but on different exchanges (interexchange spreads); or buying one futures contract such as soybeans and selling a related, but different one, such as soybean oil (intermarket spread). Spread speculators study the markets in the hopes of taking advantages of price anomalies between different maturities, different markets or different types of a similar commodity. The spread trade tracks the difference between the price of whichever commodity the trader is long in against the one he is short in. The risk is not the price of the commodity, but rather the fluctuation in the difference between the two prices. Spread trading offers less risk than trading "naked" (the actual commodity) futures because the long and short legs of the spread are correlated so in essence they hedge one another. There are lower margin requirements for spread trades, for this very reason.

Together, these speculative traders give the commodity markets the necessary liquidity that allows for the efficient operation of these markets. When there is an unaccounted for price discrepancy, these locals jump into the market and try to take advantage of the discrepancy. This usually brings markets back into efficiency. However, as electronic trading becomes more and more widespread, it is becoming difficult for the local scalpers to take advantage of these discrepancies and they are becoming a scarce commodity themselves.

Funds

Funds are institutional buyers that are made up of brokerage houses that specialize in commodities or large fund managers who hold positions in commodities to balance their portfolios. Pension funds, insurance companies and endowment funds have in recent years increased their investments in energy, metals, agricultural and other commodities and now hold significant positions in commodities. Most of these funds are invested in commodity related companies and indexes that are passively managed, but some bolder institutions, such as the Harvard University Endowment fund actively manages its commodity investments. The appeal of these investments as part of the funds' portfolios has grown because of the recent surge in commodities prices. The Goldman Sachs Commodity Index, for example, grew by 264% from its inception in 1970 through the end of 2007. Institutional investors are as anxious to increase their yields as anyone else, but were traditionally hamstrung by the aura of risk that commodities carried about them. But studies are indicating that investing in commodities may infer about the same risk as other investments. A major study by K. Geert Rouwenhorst of the Yale School of Management International Center for Finance and Gary B. Gorton of the University of Pennsylvania, Finance Department ("Facts and Fantasies about Commodity Futures" Yale ICF Working Paper No. 04-20, February 28, 2005) concluded that during the prior 45 years, commodity futures had about the same return as stocks with less risk, have outperformed bonds and are a better hedge against inflation than either stocks or bonds. (See Chapter Three for further discussions of investing in commodities as an inflation hedge.) As investing in commodities becomes more mainstream, institutions are becoming more important players in this arena. Because of the size of the trades they engage in, they usually have a strong influence on a market's direction. Even institutional funds that are passively invested exert a very strong influence, since each market trade is exaggerated by the weight of the massive dollar amounts invested.

Commercials

Commercials are large buyers or sellers who are usually hedging their physical position in that commodity. They actually produce or process the commodities that are traded in the markets and include a wide range of companies including grain merchants, food processors, livestock marketers, foreign exchange brokers, banks, oil companies and many others. "Commercials" is an actual classification by the Commodity Futures Trading Commission (CFTC) and refers to traders that use the futures market primarily to hedge their business activities. Commercials account for most of the trading in commodity markets. In the grain markets, the two sides of a commercial trade would be a farmer growing wheat and the big flour processor who is going to make it into bread, or the local orange grower and the Coca Cola, the owner of Minute Maid Orange Juice, who is going to produce the orange juice. Commercials need the futures markets, and therefore they need the various types of speculators we discussed above in order to hedge major price swings in the commodities that they produce or process. Commercials and speculators are in a symbiotic relationship; they need each other and the market would not be able to function without both of them. Mark Lundeen, an investor in the precious metals market who did an excellent study on the role of the "commercials" (A New Look at the Commercial Traders, August 2005) put it very succinctly: "The commercials need the commodities but not the price swings. The speculators need the price swings but not the commodities."

The commercials' positions are very carefully watched. They are very close to their markets and are most attuned to both short term events and long term trends that will affect them. They are viewed as having inside information about conditions in his company or in the market before the rest of the market or the media does. Commercial traders are one of the few groups on any exchange that can legally trade on inside information. An increase in long positions by the commercials in a given commodity means that these knowledgeable traders have some good insights that say the price is on the rise. Speculators follow the moves of the commercials since they usually indicate either a trend in a market or a reversal. Their positions are reported to the public by the Commodity Futures Trading Commission.

Now that we know who the players are, the next question is: What is all that frenzied activity about anyway? Spend some time viewing an exchange floor and the main things you notice are the different colored jackets speeding by, hand signals flying so fast they are blurred, and, above all, the noise.

The trading clerks, who handle all the orders on the exchange floors, wear different colored jackets to represent the clearing firm they are with. The hand signals each have their own significance and infuse three important elements into the trading: speed, efficiency, and confidentiality. Hand signals are fast (speed), they can be seen when voices cannot be heard (efficiency), and you don't have to have papers showing who is ordering a trade (confidentiality).

These are the qualities that are trumpeted by those who are still opposed to completely electronic commodity trading.

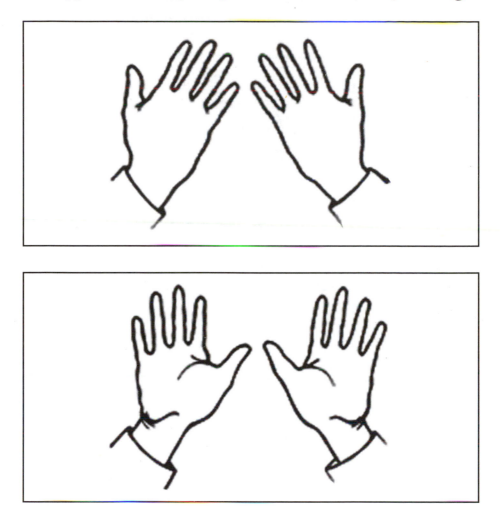

Buy Signal: Palms in ("I'm a buyer")
Sell Signal: Palms out ("I'm a seller")

Quantities are indicated by the number of fingers, and where the fingers are placed indicates multiples: one through nine, they will touch their chins; multiples of ten, they will touch their foreheads with their fingers; multiples of one hundred they will touch their foreheads with their fists. It gets even more complicated than that, with expiry month of the contract desired, whether an order has been filled, and so on. Here is the unsurprising signal to cancel an order:

But do not worry, the trader or broker on the floor is the only one who has to worry about remembering these signals, and you can be assured that they know and use them perfectly, since making a mistake with any one of them can mean a big loss for a broker. If the topic fascinates you, or if you want to understand the signals a little better before you go for a visit to the floor, get a copy of "An Introduction to Hand Signals" published by the Chicago Mercantile Exchange.

The noise on the trading floor comes from the method of trading called "open outcry" and distinguishes commodity trading from stock trading. Commodity prices are not set at a futures market; the price is a function of what a buyer is willing to pay and what a seller is willing to accept. The "open outcry" system enables buyers and sellers to hear all available bids and offers — similar to an auction but in this case every trader is also his own auctioneer.

ELECTRONIC MARKETS

Recently, electronic markets have been spreading at the expense of these traditional open outcry trading floors. Whereas just a few years ago, all futures trading took place in the open outcry pits, today the volume in physical commodities (such as agricultural commodities and oils) are still traded by the open outcry method, while the rest of the world's trading markets are purely electronic. The traditional rough-and-tumble culture of trading in the pits is giving way to the less frenetic form of trading via computer, and electronic trading does not depend on a specific locations or having the loudest voice. It only depends on advanced technology.

Joseph Shatz, government/financial futures and options strategist at Merrill Lynch in New York, said, "I wouldn't be surprised if pit trading didn't exist in a few years." As more electronic exchanges, such as BrokerTec, enter the financial futures market, the trend will continue. Competition is arising in many forms, including entirely electronic exchanges as well as exchange-traded funds, such as the fixed-income ETFs or iShares.

In 1989, the Commodity Futures Trading Commission approved a global computer-trading network, Globex, which enables the futures and options trading markets to operate electronically after regular trading hours. The Globex system, developed by the Chicago Mercantile Exchange and Reuters Holding PLC, represented the first alternative to the futures industry's open outcry system of trading.

The open outcry system had been under increased scrutiny; critics contend that the old system of processing orders by hand signals and manual note taking has created the potential for widespread trading abuses. In addition, advances in electronic monitoring systems have made trading infinitely faster and the controls are easier to monitor than in the old system. The Globex system is less vulnerable to market disruptions as well. Orders on Globex are matched by computer on the basis of time and price. As soon as a match is made, the trade is confirmed on the originating terminal and electronically posted. In addition, Globex enables the markets to operate electronically after regular trading hours, creating a global 24-hour trading day. In regular business hours, traders can continue to use the open outcry system "It is a regulator's dream," said Leo Melamed, chairman of the Merc's executive committee. "It provides a perfect audit trail."

CASE STUDY: RENÉ MARCHAND

What are the qualities you need to successfully trade commodities?

Diligence, patience, discipline and the ability to act upon information in a quick and decisive manner.

Which commodities do you prefer to trade and why?

Any market that is liquid, with good open interest. The Agricultural Futures and Options on Futures Contracts have always been a favorite of mine. There are lots of factors that go into determining price and its fun to dissect what specific factors are influencing prices at any given point in time.

Are there certain markets you won't trade in?

I mostly stay with US exchange traded futures.

What is your favorite (or has been most successful) strategy?

CASE STUDY: RENÉ MARCHAND

Let me start of by saying that there is no one strategy that works all of the time. As a trader you have to realize this and adapt your trading style to the current market characteristics. As of late, Trend trading has been working because of many world factors and inflation. This can and no doubt will change.

What's the hardest thing to do or decision to make in trading?

Knowing when to exit a losing trade.

Do you rely on fundamentals or technical analysis more?

Most of my work is technical in nature, but traders need to know the underlying fundamentals impacting prices. I would say I'm 75 % technical, 20% fundamental and after years of trading, 5 % intuitive.

Which technical indicator do you rely on the most?

It depends on the nature of the trade. Is it a Day Trade, Position Trade, Spread Trade, or an option play? In basic position trades, the key building block indicators that I use are the 18 day and 45 day moving average of closes. I use much shorter term indicators when Day Trading.

Do you trade full time or part time? Can a part time trader have real success?

I am a full time broker who works with and helps other traders, both those with experience and those with little if any experience in trading. I do believe that a part time trader can have success. In fact the vast majority who trade are most likely Part Time Traders.

What are your best knowledge resources?

The internet and reliable information from a good news resource.

What was your most successful trade?

Long Gold and Crude Oil this past year.

Least successful?

Selling Wheat this past year.

What do you think right now about:

Oil: Still Bullish

Wheat: Topping Out

Corn: More upside, after the current break

CASE STUDY: RENÉ MARCHAND

Beans: Near term profit targets have been reached. Look for corrective break to catch as fundamentals remain solid.

Coffee: I wouldn't be surprised to see $2.00

Gold: Easy money may have been made, but with US Dollar free fall, Gold is still bullish. Look for challenge of $1000-$1050, then some consolidation.

Dollar: Bearish until the Fed stops cutting rates.

What's the most interesting/funny/strange story you have that is related to commodities trading?

A $7,000 Account opened with me in September of 2007. The client really didn't know much about trading but got long Grains, Metals, Energies and Softs. The account went over $250,000 this week. Though not common, you have to love stories like this.

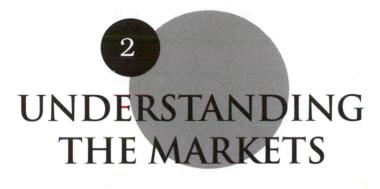

UNDERSTANDING THE MARKETS

"Education is the progressive discovery of our own ignorance."

— *Will Durant*

Unlike other investments in a portfolio, commodity trading takes special skill and risk tolerance. Every investor realizes that every investment has a risk, and the higher the risk, the higher the rewards. The ideal solution is to have a balanced portfolio that includes some very conservative investments such as CDs and mutual funds (which have smaller returns, but work better to preserve capital), mixed with some investments that have a higher potential return, along with higher risk, such as commodities. As we will see, including commodities is an ideal way to assure that one's portfolio is balanced in terms of risk, return and inflation protection.

How much of a portfolio should be devoted to commodities is a very personal decision, one that is influenced by risk tolerance and time commitment. Obviously, owning CDs and mutual funds does not involve too much of either, and the reward reflects that. There is very little risk since bank CDs are insured by the Federal Deposit Insurance Corporation (FDIC) and there is not much of a time commitment involved in managing a portfolio of CDs, outside of calling banks (or researching on the internet) for the best rates. Owning commodities involves recognizing and taking risk, and being actively involved in the management of "positions": how much of each commodity one holds. (There are exceptions; a managed commodity account can theoretically be managed with very little involvement by the investor and commodity indices are intended to be passive, long-term investments.) A neophyte in commodities may choose to start small, perhaps with a small percentage of the overall portfolio, and test the waters. Success breeds success, so most successful traders will gradually increase their positions.

One of the best first steps in becoming involved in the commodity markets is self-education. There are many excellent books on learning about commodity trading. See the Bibliography, and do additional independent research. Start by reading and following the daily markets to observe and learn about the market movements. Read The Wall Street Journal or New York Times for their commodity news sections. Learn the symbols for each of the commodities you may be interested in, and follow their progress. Very similar to the reports on the price fluctuations of stocks, the fluctuations in each commodity are reported with price headings. Or you can go right to the site of the Exchange the commodity is traded on. Here is what the performance of corn futures looked like in The Wall Street Journal after the close on May 4, 2007:

	OPEN	HIGH	LOW	SETTLE	CHG	INTEREST
May	380.00	382.75	376.25	381.25	+1.50	11,259
July	389.75	393.00	385.75	390.75	+1.50	492,659

The column heads are pretty self explanatory: the first column is the opening price, next is the highest price it went to, then the lowest, and the price it ended or "settled" at and how much of a change that represents over the previous day's close. Open interest is the number of contracts that are outstanding in that position. The higher prices for the July contract tells us that the market expects prices to go higher, and the wide discrepancy between open interest in May versus July is due to the fact that May is the current trading month and positions are being settled and falling off the board.

To decide whether to begin trading, you have to find a source for prices so that you can follow their movements. Many large daily newspapers have a commodities price section, but financial publications such as The Wall Street Journal, Investor's Business Daily or the Financial Times will have a much more comprehensive section. Investor's Business Daily shows price movements on a chart, which makes it much easier for a trader to understand in a graphic view what is happening in a market. As we will see later, charts are very important to traders for many reasons other than following the reported price of a commodity.

For anyone who wants almost up-to-the-minute price fluctuations to get a feel for the market, CNN is a perfect solution. In the streaming information on the bottom of the screen, prices of commodities are shown every ten minutes during the day, after the headline "Commodities." You have to know the codes used to represent each commodity. Most of them are fairly logical: C for corn, NG for natural gas, G for gold. Each trading month has its own abbreviation, though these do not follow the same logic as the names of the commodities: K for May, N for July, U for September.

COMMODITY	ABBREV.	EXCHANGE	TRADING MONTHS
Corn	C	Chicago Board of Trade	Dec, Mar, May, Jul, Sep
Oats	O	Chicago Board of Trade	Jul, Sep, Dec, Mar, May
Soybeans	S	Chicago Board of Trade	Sep, Nov, Jan, Mar, May, Jul, Aug
Soybean Meal	SM	Chicago Board of Trade	Oct, Dec, Jan, Mar, May, Jul, Aug, Sep
Soybean Oil	BO	Chicago Board of Trade	Oct, Dec, Jan, Mar, May, Jul, Aug, Sep
Rough Rice	RR	Chicago Board of Trade	Sep, Nov, Jan, Mar, May, Jul
Wheat	W	Chicago Board of Trade	Jul, Sep, Dec, Mar, May
Barley	AB	Winnipeg Commodity Exchange	Mar, May, Jul, Oct, Dec
Canola	RS	Winnipeg Commodity Exchange	Jan, Mar, May, Jul, Sep, Nov
Cattle-Live	LC	Chicago Mercantile Exch.	Feb, Apr, Jun, Aug, Oct, Dec
Lean Hogs	LH	Chicago Mercantile Exch	Feb, Apr, May, Jun, Jul, Aug, Oct, Dec
Lumber	LB	Chicago Mercantile Exch	Jan, Mar, May, Jul, Sep, Nov
Cocoa	CC	Coffee, Sugar, Cocoa Exch.	Mar, May, Jul, Sep, Dec
Coffee	KC	Coffee, Sugar, Cocoa Exch	Mar, May, Jul, Sep, Dec
Sugar	SB	Coffee, Sugar, Cocoa Exch	Mar, May, Jul, Oct
Cotton	CT	New York Cotton Exch.	Mar, May, Jul, Oct, Dec

In general, some of the commodities are grouped. The agriculturals include wheat, corn, soybeans, etc; sugar, coffee, cocoa, and orange juice are called "softs" or "tropicals"; and metals and oils are lumped together.

Month Abbreviations

- January-F
- February-G
- March-H
- April-J
- May-K
- June-M
- July-N
- August-Q
- September-U
- October-V
- November-X
- December-Z

You should also be aware of how the price quoting systems differ. The agricultural commodities are quoted on the CNN ticker with an extra decimal place. Therefore, even though the May opening for corn is quoted at $380.00, this does not mean that corn is $380 per bushel. Because the price fluctuations can be fairly small, the extra decimals are used to allow for this, and $380.00 translates as $3.80. On the other hand, the commodities that are the most expensive are quoted with fewer decimal points, since the hundreds of dollars change so rarely, and space is needed to reflect the fluctuations in cents, tens of cents and dollars. June gold, for instance, may be quoted on the ticker, for sake of space, at GM 84.20. Since all traders know that gold is trading in the $600 range, they also know that this means the June gold quote is $684.20.

One of the best ways to get a feel for the market is to start a dummy commodity portfolio. While people tend to take greater risks and ride losses longer when real money is not at stake, it will give a "wanna be" trader experience in watching the markets, spotting trends, seeing which kinds of influences act upon the markets most strongly, how the exchanges work, etc.

Clearly, hypothetical performance results are limited and should only be used as a learning tool. Doing well in your mock trading account is not a good measure of your future performance, since when real money is not at stake, greater risks may be taken.

At the outset, learning the basics is still critical. And it is far better to learn these lessons when there is no money at risk. Thoroughly read up on the commodity markets and only then, when you feel that you are knowledgeable enough to start investing in commodities, should you call a broker to get started. If you are new to trading commodities, it is probably best to start with a full-service broker. A full-service broker can give you a valuable education in commodities trading that you can build on over time. He will also help you avoid many of the foolish and avoidable mistakes new traders frequently make and help you to spot trends, one of the most important components in trading commodities. For all of this education and advice, you will of course have to pay more than you would for a discount broker, but this extra price may prove more valuable than its cost in the long run.

PLACING ORDERS WITH A BROKER

There are different types of orders a trader can give a broker, and there are differing procedures that accompany each type of order. It is not as simple as just buy or sell, and for a good reason. No trader wants to let the price run away from him without any control in the interim. So there are many types of both buy and sell orders: limit orders, market orders (which are also called contingency orders), market if touched orders, and stop orders.

Limit orders

If a trader wants to buy a commodity at a certain price, or less, or sell a commodity at a certain price, or more, he will enter a limit order. This means that if the price goes above the limit (for a buy order) or below the limit (for a sell order), the order is automatically cancelled. There are "or better" limit orders for the cases when the market moves quickly to and above (or below) the price specified, and the order can be filled at this more advantageous price. In other words, the trader "limits" his loss on the order because it cannot go above or below a level that he sets. However, since the broker cannot pay more than the limit on a buy order or less than the limit on a sell order, if the market never reaches those levels, the trade may never be executed. Even if the market briefly touched your level, someone else's order may be filled before it resumes an upward climb.

Market orders

This is the fastest and easiest trade for a broker to execute. This order tells a broker that the buy or sell order should be entered at whatever the price is at the current time. The rule is that it must be filled within three minutes, so it is a time-sensitive order, rather than a price-sensitive order such as a limit order. In the market, a trader buys at the offer price and sells at the bid price. The bid is the price put out for immediate purchase and the offer is the price at which a seller is offering for immediate sale. Using a market order guarantees that your order is filled, since there is no set criteria in terms of price-when the order goes through, the commodity will be bought or sold.

Market If Touched Orders (MIT)

This order works like a limit order except that if you are trying to sell a commodity at a certain price, as with a limit order, and the market goes up and touches that price, your order is filled at the market. In other words, your order does not necessarily have to be filled at the price you wanted, but it will be filled when the market first hits the price you specified, even if it continues above (for a buy) or below (for a sell). Usually a trader uses this kind of order when he has fixed a number at which he is interested in taking a profit. Even if the order cannot be filled at the exact price specified, it is filled relatively shortly thereafter. On average, MITs tend to be filled better than stops because you are moving with the prevailing trend. An MIT could also be used to initiate a new short position above the market. Or an MIT can be used to buy when it is placed under the market to exit a short position or enter a new long. For example, if the market price of your commodity was at 100, you would place an MIT to buy at 99 if you wanted to be long the commodity, but you would place a stop to sell at 99 if you wanted to be short.

Market on close orders (MOC)

When you place a market on close order, you are not selecting a specific price but instead a specific time to execute your order. Your order is executed at whatever price that commodity reaches at the close of the trading session for that day or within the closing range of prices for that day. This is an order that is filled during the final seconds of trading at whatever price is available at that time. An MOC order can be submitted at any time within a trading session, but it is only executable at closing, at the closing price. Most floor brokers reserve the right to refuse an MOC order up to 15 minutes before the close, depending upon market conditions. Frequently, MOC orders are used by day traders to assure that they will not end up holding a position overnight.

Stop Orders

Stop orders are orders to sell or buy based on the loss the trader is willing to accept. This is to manage losses and is also called a "stop-loss order." Sometimes "slippage" may occur, since a stop-loss order is mandated to be filled within five minutes, but if the market is moving quickly, that may not be possible and the final price may be somewhat higher or lower than the order. Stop orders can be used to minimize the potential loss in a position, or to protect a profit on an existing position.

Stop Close Only Orders

If you choose a stop close only order, your stop order is

executed only at the close of trading and only if the closing trading range is at or through your designated stop price. It might be considered a hybrid of the market on close order and the stop order. A disadvantage of this type of order may be that it may be filled at an undesirable price, especially in a volatile market.

Stop Limit Order

A stop limit order is a combination of both a stop order and a limit order. Once the stop price is reached, the order becomes a limit order and the transaction is executed only if the specified price at which you want the order to be executed has been reached. The main advantage of a stop limit order is that the trader can control the price at which the trade will be executed. However, as with all limit orders, the risk is that the trade may never be filled because the commodity never reaches the limit price. This can happen most frequently in very volatile markets with wide price swings.

One Cancels the Other (OCO)

OCO stands for one cancels the other. It is used either to take profits or cut losses. Here is an example. If you have bought soybeans at 735.00, you may have decided to take your profits at 739.00, or cut your losses if the market goes down to 730.00. You would then place an order with your broker to sell at 739.00 or 730.00 stop: one order cancels the other order. This way, you are assured that if one side is hit, the other side is cancelled. This is a very important type of order in extremely volatile markets. If you had two separate orders, when the market runs up to 739.00, you would take your profit, but when it traded down to 730.00, you would be in a short position that you may not want to be in.

Good Till Cancelled (CTC)

This is not actually a type of order, but an additional instruction, since, regardless of the type of order that is placed with a broker, the person initiating the trade has to decide whether or not to make it a "GTC", or Good Till Cancelled Order. Whatever order you give to your broker, if it is not met under the conditions you set, it will stand. If you decide that the market is moving the wrong way all together, you may decide you want to get out of an order, but you have to take the extra step to cancel it. A GTC order will be in place not matter what, unless you specifically cancel it. This is a very important concept in trading. Do not forget which positions you have out there. If you do not have the time to review them and cancel or renew them very frequently, you want to avoid having GTC orders.

MARGIN

The concept of margins is simple. "Ya gotta put yer money down" before you can enter the game. Margins serve the purpose of a performance guarantee so that the clearinghouse your broker is dealing with has the funds from you to cover any of your trades. Here is the official definition of the term from the Glossary of Terms published by the New York Mercantile Exchange:

"The amount of money or collateral deposited by a customer with his broker, or deposited by a broker with a clearing member, or by a clearing member with the clearinghouse, for the purpose of insuring the broker or clearinghouse against adverse price movement on open futures contracts. The margin is not partial payment on a purchase. 1) Initial margin is the minimum deposit per contract required when a futures position is opened. 2) Maintenance margin is a sum which must be maintained on deposit at all times. If the equity in a customer's account drops to, or under, that level because of an adverse price movement, the clearing member must issue a margin call to restore the customer's equity. Margins are set by the Exchange based on its analysis of risk volatility in the market at that time."

Everyone trader involved in the market is also putting up this same kind of deposit so that the market constantly has the flow of funds to operate. If the players in the market were not able to meet their obligations, the market would collapse. Each exchange sets its own minimums for margins, called the "exchange minimum." In addition, brokers can and do set additional margins for their customers. The more volatile the market, the higher the margin is likely to be. At the time of this book's writing (May 2007), the natural gas and crude oil markets are currently the most volatile and therefore have initial margins ranging from $2,475 to more than $7,000, and maintenance margins ranging from $2,250 to $6,000 per contract. Compare that to soybean oil on the Chicago Mercantile Exchange at $608 and $450, respectively. As market conditions change, the Exchanges review the risk volatility and reset margins accordingly.

Let us assume a trader wants to get his feet wet with a less volatile (and therefore lower margin requirement) commodity such as soybean oil. He would have to deposit an initial margin of $608 per contract to start a trading position. In addition, he would have to deposit $450 per contract as a maintenance margin. This amount has to be on deposit in his margin account at all times. If any trade he makes brings this amount below the required margins, the trader would receive a "margin call" to deposit more funds and bring his account back to the required level. Therefore, if he put $1,058 into his account, he can buy 1 soybean oil contract. If the price of soybean oil went down, his account would be debited the necessary amount to cover the potential loss. If the price fell so far that the maintenance margin of $450 no longer covered the loss, funds would be debited, if necessary, from his initial margin account, and he would receive a margin call to bring both margin balances up to the required levels. (Actually he would get the call before it reached such a level — neither the clearinghouse nor the broker is going to take a chance on not being covered.) When the trader receives the margin call, he can deposit more margin funds or he can close out his position and take the loss. If he does not cover the account, his position is closed out by default.

There is an upside and a downside to margins. Besides adding the necessary security to the operations of the markets, it allows traders to use leverage to control larger positions than the margin account. Beware, however, since because of this leverage, a trader can become overextended and owe many thousands of dollars worth of a commodity for his small, thousand-dollar deposit. In the above example, almost $20,000 worth of soybean oil (60,000 pounds at a price of $.3305 a pound), would be controlled for $1,058.

That is the power and danger of margins, and anyone interested in trading in commodities should make sure he understands the risks. A broker should thoroughly explain the requirements, and any further information can be obtained from the relevant Exchange. Each Exchange has a section on their Web site with the margin requirements for the commodities exchanged on it, and traders can sign up for automatic notification of any changes in margin requirements.

MAKING A TRADE

Let us examine exactly what happens once you have decided to make a futures trade. You call your well-chosen broker (see Chapter Four) or log on to your account to place the order. You have decided to buy 100 July 2007 CBOT corn at market open order. This means that you want to by 100 contracts of corn futures with a maturity date of July 2007 on the Chicago Board of Trade at whatever price the market is at when the order is entered. Because it is an open order, your order will remain open for as many trading sessions as it takes to reach "a fill" (the order is able to be executed). The first thing you have to do is to deposit the margin money in your account with your broker. You will be trading on the Chicago Mercantile Exchange, the exchange that handles corn futures contracts. The initial margin requirement per contract is $1,350 and the maintenance margin requirement is $1,000, so you have to make a deposit of $235,000 to be able to buy 100 contracts of corn. (Don't forget, with this deposit of $235,000, you are controlling the equivalent value of $1,948,750.00 worth of corn.) Once the margin has been established, you call your broker with the order: "Hello, this is Trader Bob, account number 123456, buy 100 CBOT July corn at the market" Broker: "100 CBOT July corn at the market; hold please." The broker hands the order to the clerk, or it is relayed to a clerk electronically. This clerk is employed by the brokerage firm that your broker works for, or by the broker himself if he is an independent broker. The clerk's job is to take down these orders and pass them along, either electronically or physically, to a floor broker. In this case, the floor broker is on the floor of the Chicago Board of Trade, where you are placing your order. The floor broker is who most people associate with the commodities trading floor: the one gesticulating and shouting in the large ring, known as "the pit."

Each commodity has its own pit on the floor. For example, on the floor of the New York Metals Exchange (NYMEX), there will be a pit for natural gas, one for crude oil, and one for heating oil. Only the commodity of that pit can be traded in that pit. When a floor broker receives an order from his clerk, he has to find a matching order and fill the order of his client. From the shouts and gestures of the other brokers in the pit, he knows who is interested in buying or selling whatever quantity of whatever month he is selling or buying. When he has a "fill," he writes an order ticket indicating the time the trade was made. In addition to the floor brokers, floor traders will be in the pit. The floor broker is licensed to trade on behalf of clients; a floor trader can only trade for his own account. These are the traders we discussed before, who are frequently known as locals, and who play a vital role in the commodity trading industry. They provide the liquidity necessary for the system to run smoothly. The client's floor broker may trade with either another floor broker, or with a floor trader, to fulfill the order he has been given.

Now your order for 100 July Corn has been filled and the broker will confirm to you: "100 CBOT July corn bought at 389.75." Both the buyer and seller write a ticket that a trade went through, but only the seller must notify the Exchange that the transaction took place. He writes the price, quality, and quantity of the commodity and the time the transaction took place on a ticket that he gives (literally throws) to the "card clocker." The card clocker sits in the middle of the pit and has the responsibility to stamp each ticket with the time he receives it. When you see how busy the exchange floor is, it is hard to imagine how he can keep up with this barrage of tickets thrown at him.

The next person who handles your 100 contracts of corn is the floor runner. The floor runner takes all of the tickets from the card clocker and gives them to the exchange's data entry people. The title "floor runner" is quite literal. The floor runner spends the day running back and forth between the card clocker and the data entry desk. The data entry clerks enter all of the details of the trade into the exchange's data entry system. The price reporter is another employee of the exchange who reports the price of each trade. This is done right on the floor into a handheld computer and the information is immediately updated on the exchange's floor board. The news services, such as Dow Jones and Reuters, relay these prices immediately to their clients. If you are not a subscriber to a news service, the price you will see on the computer will be delayed by about 15 minutes. The news services pay to receive the prices immediately and charge for subscriptions to their clients to receive this information almost as instantaneously.

All of this action is under the supervision of the pit supervisor. The supervisor is there to make sure that each trader is following the rules and that all of the action in the pit is running smoothly. Despite the seeming chaos on the floor, the situation is under complete control at all times, and the supervisor is the one who makes sure of this. All of the activity involved in filling your order took place seamlessly, and in a very short time; the only evidence of flailing arms, screaming voices, flying tickets, and dashing runners will be the confirmation number that the trade has been executed. You now own 100 contracts of corn for delivery in July 2007. Don't worry, you won't have to buy a big popcorn popper for all of that corn; the idea is to watch the price of July corn increase and to take advantage of this price increase to earn a profit. This market is used by speculators (that now includes you) who are interested in making a profit, or hedgers who want some insurance against adverse price increases or decreases. The cash or spot market is the market where the actual corn is bought and sold for use as animal feed or in consumer products. This "cash market" is used by those companies or individuals who actually buy or sell the physical commodity.

After your order has been processed in this frenzy, you want to protect yourself from runaway losses by entering a stop loss on this order. You inform your broker that you would like to enter a stop order: "Good till cancelled, sell 100 July CBOT corn at 385.00 stop." The broker will confirm: "For account 123456, sell 100 July CBOT corn at 385.00

stop, good till cancelled." This sell order gives the broker instructions to automatically sell these corn contracts in case the price falls to 385.00. If July corn does not go up to 395.00, as hoped, at least you limit the loss to $23,750, since your will sell your contracts at 395.00 (5,000 bushels per contract x 100 contracts x $.0475 loss per contract). You do not have to be hanging on the phone to call the broker when the loss becomes too great; the broker already has the order. If you are correct about your feel for the market, and the price increases to 395.00, and you sell at that level, you have a profit of $26,250. Once the price has increased to a certain extent, of course, you can lift the stop and place a new one at a higher level, thus locking in a profit in case prices increase and then start falling.

HOW PRICES ARE DETERMINED

How are futures prices determined? Consider the alternative to obtaining the commodity in the future: simply wait and purchase the commodity in the future spot market. Since the future spot price cannot be known today, a futures contract is the means to lock in the price of a future trade transaction. In determining the fair futures price, market participants compare the current futures price to the spot price that can be expected to prevail at the maturity of the futures contract. In other words, futures markets look to the future and the futures price includes expectations about the future spot price. If spot prices are expected to be much higher at the maturity of the futures contract than they are today, the current futures price is set at a high level relative to the current spot price. By the same token, lower expected spot prices in the future are reflected in a low current futures price. This is a simplistic view, and there are a great many factors that influence the relationship between spot and futures prices as we shall see. Prices in general are determined by supply and demand; prices of commodities are additionally influenced by weather, politics, regulations and the economic strength of a given producing region versus that of the consuming region. For the sake of this explanation, however, we will keep the simplistic view.

Since foreseeable trends in spot markets all become a part of the price determination mechanism when the futures price is set, expected movements in the spot price are not a source of return to an investor in the futures market. Investors in futures profit when the spot price at maturity turns out to be higher than expected when they entered into the contract, and lose when the spot price is lower than originally anticipated. An investor in a futures contract bets on the future spot price, and by entering into a futures contract assumes the risk of any unexpected movements in the future spot price. Any deviation from this expected future spot price is completely unpredictable, and should average out to zero over the long range for investors. That is, unless the investor has an ability to correctly time the market more times than he does not.

This is called the Efficient Market Hypothesis. In 2003, economist Eugene Fama was nominated for the Nobel Prize in economics for work pertaining to his efficient-market hypothesis, which states that a free and open market adjusts its prices almost instantaneously to all publicly available information. That suggests that one cannot predictably and consistently outperform market returns through fundamental or technical analysis of publicly available information. The market reacts quickly and efficiently, whether the information is right or not, and it continues to react and readjust almost instantaneously and pretty much constantly. Fama's studies concentrated on the stock market, but what is considered publicly available information in the stock market is different from the commodities market, especially since the distribution of corporate information is regulated so differently than commodities market information.

If this is the case, then, how can the average investor in the commodities markets hope to earn a return if he (1) cannot benefit from expected spot price movements and (2) he is not able to outsmart or predict the market? The answer to this is the risk premium, which is the difference between the current futures price and the expected future spot price. If the futures price of a commodity today is set below the expected future spot price, a purchase of futures will, on average, earn money. If the futures price is above the expected future spot price, a seller of futures will earn a risk premium.

Speculators would provide this insurance and buy futures, but they would demand a futures price below the spot price that could be expected to exist at the maturity of the futures contract. This is the concept of backwardation. By "backwardating" the futures price relative to the expected future spot price, speculators would receive a risk premium from producers for assuming the risk of future price fluctuations. One can almost view it as an insurance company earning the premiums on a homeowner or auto insurance policy because the homeowner or car owner does not want to take a chance on replacing the asset if an accident occurs.

Why will a buyer or seller of futures earn a risk premium? Famed economist Maynard Keynes' theory of normal backwardation states that the risk premium would accrue to the buyers of futures. He expected that producers of commodities would seek to hedge the price risk of their output. For example, a producer of grain would sell grain futures to lock in the future price of his crops and obtain insurance against the price risk of the grain at harvest. This is the heart of the futures market concept. How is the risk premium earned? Do speculators have to hold the futures contract until expiration? The answer is no. Over time, as the maturity date of the futures contract draws close, the futures price will start to approach the spot price of a commodity. At maturity, the futures contract will become equivalent to a spot contract, and the futures price will equal the spot price. If futures prices were initially set below the expected future spot price, the futures price will gradually increase over time, rewarding the long position.

Whether Keynes' theory of normal backwardation is an accurate predictor of the determination of the futures price is a matter that is constantly under study by economists, but the above discussion of the mechanics of futures markets gives us some important insight into investment in the futures markets. First of all, the expected payoff to a futures position is the risk premium. The actual payoff is the risk premium plus any unexpected deviation of the future spot price from the expected future spot price. Next, if a futures price is set below the expected future spot price, the futures prices will tend to rise over time, providing a return to investors in futures. The expected trends in spot prices are not what creates a return to an investor in futures.

Let us look at a market example. Assume that the spot price of oil is $60 per barrel and that the participants in the market expect the price to be $57 in three months. For investors to be interested in this market, the futures price should be set at $55, which is at a discount to the anticipated future spot price. The difference between the futures price and the anticipated future spot price, or $2, is the risk premium that the investor expects to earn for taking in this short-term price risk.

Now suppose that when the contract expires, oil is trading at the expected price of $57. If someone had invested in the physical commodity, and therefore cared about the direction of spot prices, he has just lost $3 ($60 - $57). An investor in the futures contract, however, would have gained the difference between the final spot price of $57 and the initial futures price of $55, or $2.

The example above examines the case where the anticipated future spot price of $57 is actually the case. But suppose the future price of $57 is not realized and instead the final spot price turns out to be $56. In this case, the realized return to the investor would be $1. This realized return can be broken down into the risk premium ($57 - $55 = $2), less the difference between the final spot price and the expected price ($56 - $55 = $1).

This example illustrates the essential benefit of the performance of commodity futures prices over the performance of spot commodity prices. The return for an investment in commodity futures exceeds the return to a holder of spot commodities. Commodity spot prices and commodity futures returns have to outpace inflation, and the return on the futures position is closely linked with movements in the spot. An investment in commodity futures will benefit from unexpected increases in spot prices. Especially in times of high spot market volatility, the returns to spot and futures will be highly correlated. The spot index includes trends in the spot price, which are excluded from the futures index. In turn the futures index rises with the risk free rate plus any risk premium earned by the futures position.

INVESTMENT PHILOSOPHIES

Two of the most important concepts of creating consistently successful trading positions in commodities is to understand and determine an investment philosophy and an investment plan. A trader needs to be clear on what he hopes to gain from his participation in the commodities market, and switching plans strategies and plans constantly will only erode his position. There are some popular and valuable overall strategies that some traders use as the cornerstone of their trading philosophy. They are value investing, hedging, and diversification.

Value Investing

Value investing attempts to identify those assets that are

undervalued and take advantage of a supposedly inevitable rise in their price. Value investing, at its core, is buying low and selling high, but it does not assume that just because the price of a commodity is low in relative or historic terms that the price will rise. This is a concept that is a strong underpinning of investments in the stock market, and the concept applies in the commodities markets as well. There has to be a reason for the value to increase. When we examine the price of coffee and its prospects, one of the first things that is noted is that coffee prices have not kept up with the general upward trend in commodity prices. Does this mean coffee is a value investment and is bound to rise? Unfortunately, coffee supply has exceeded demand and this has kept prices down. A value investor would have to find sufficient evidence that supply is decreasing while demand is increasing to support a strong position in the coffee market. Of course, in the case of commodities, one can ride the opposite wave of value investing and look for commodities that are poised to fall in price and take short positions in them. But in either case, it is the inherent value in the asset that has to be examined in order to build an investing strategy such as this.

Hedging

A trader can hedge his position in a number of ways, and while it may limit profits, it will certainly also prevent runaway losses. Some people use stop-loss orders to protect themselves against adverse moves. A stop order is placed so that a trade is automatically executed when a certain price is reached. For example, if you are holding a position in May corn at 380.00, anticipating an increase to 389.00, you may want to limit your loss. To do so, you put in a stop-loss order at 375.00, so that you know the maximum you will lose on this trade. If the price continues to increase, you will ride the increase until you reach your desired price or take your profit somewhere on the way to it, but you don't have to worry about the market plummeting on you, since your position will automatically be liquidated at 375.00. Other traders prefer to use options to hedge a position. Options are a complex and widely used instrument for both hedging risk and earning profits, but it is such a broad and complicated topic that it requires a study all its own. In this book, we will supply the following basic explanation.

Options are contracts that give buyers the right, but not the obligation, to buy or sell a given commodity, in exchange for the payment of a premium. The buyer of a call option has the right to buy (or call for) a commodity. The buyer of a put option has the right to sell (or put for sale) a commodity. (There are also compound options, which consist of combinations of puts and calls, and other combinations and complexities in this market.) If a trader buys a call option to hedge a short position, he will pay a premium to exercise the option. This means that he can "trade in" the long options position against his short futures position and only have to pay whatever fee (premium). His loss is limited to the cost of the premium.

Diversification

Another protective strategy is diversification. This involves buying a range of investments in an area of commodities that one finds interesting, for example, futures in addition to the equity of a company in that field, and perhaps also a managed fund that holds positions in that commodity. Diversified commodity indices have recently shown an excellent record of outperforming individual commodity prices and futures; the Standard and Poors GSCI discussed earlier is only one example of these successful funds. Diversified commodity indices provide investors a way to add commodities to their portfolios without having to pay the heavy expenses charged by actively managed commodities funds. In addition, these futures based funds bundle many commodities together and allow investors to spread out risk rather than invest in individual futures contracts or trying to create their own futures portfolios. Although these EFTs (exchange traded funds) can invest in a single commodity, most of them are broader based and invest in many different commodities. If the purpose of investing in one of these funds is diversification to limit risk, rather than just investment performance improvement, it would make more sense to invest in a fund that contains a wide range of commodities. It is also important to understand the weighting system that is being used by the fund. A system that uses total dollar amount traded, for example, may be heavily weighted towards the oil complex, and therefore some of the diversification benefit may be lost.

CASE STUDY: BOYD BAKER

What are the qualities you need to successfully trade commodities?

Diligence, patience, discipline and the ability to act upon information in a quick and decisive manner.

CASE STUDY: BOYD BAKER

Which commodities do you prefer to trade and why?

Any market that is liquid, with good open interest. The Agricultural Futures and Options on Futures Contracts have always been a favorite of mine. There are lots of factors that go into determining price and its fun to dissect what specific factors are influencing prices at any given point in time.

Are there certain markets you won't trade in?

I mostly stay with US exchange traded futures.

What is your favorite (or has been most successful) strategy?

Let me start of by saying that there is no one strategy that works all of the time. As a trader you have to realize this and adapt your trading style to the current market characteristics. As of late, Trend trading has been working because of many world factors and inflation. This can and no doubt will change.

What's the hardest thing to do or decision to make in trading?

Knowing when to exit a losing trade.

Do you rely on fundamentals or technical analysis more?

Most of my work is technical in nature, but traders need to know the underlying fundamentals impacting prices. I would say I'm 75% technical, 20% fundamental and after years of trading, 5% intuitive.

Which technical indicator do you rely on the most?

It depends on the nature of the trade. Is it a Day Trade, Position Trade, Spread Trade, or an option play? In basic position trades, the key building block indicators that I use are the 18 day and 45 day moving average of closes. I use much shorter term indicators when Day Trading.

Do you trade full time or part time? Can a part time trader have real success?

I am a full time broker who works with and helps other traders, both those with experience and those with little if any experience in trading. I do believe that a part time trader can have success. In fact the vast majority who trade are most likely Part Time Traders.

What are your best knowledge resources?

The internet and reliable information from a good news resource.

CASE STUDY: BOYD BAKER

Long Gold and Crude Oil this past year.

Least successful?

Selling Wheat this past year.

What do you think right now about:

Oil: Still Bullish

Wheat: Topping Out

Corn: More upside, after the current break

Beans: Near term profit targets have been reached. Look for corrective break to catch as fundamentals remain solid.

Coffee: I wouldn't be surprised to see $2.00

Gold: Easy money may have been made, but with US Dollar free fall, Gold is still bullish. Look for challenge of $1,000-$1,050, then some consolidation.

Dollar: Bearish until the Fed stops cutting rates.

What's the most interesting/funny/strange story you have that is related to commodities trading?

A $7,000 Account opened with me in September of 2007. The client really didn't know much about trading but got long Grains, Metals, Energies and Softs. The account went over $250,000 this week. Though not common, you have to love stories like this

3

THE WHYS OF COMMODITY TRADING

"Every truth passes through three stages before it is recognized. First it is ridiculed, then it is opposed and then it is regarded as self-evident."

— Arthur Schopenhauer

One of the biggest attractions of commodity trading is the possibility of making large profits from small investments. This is done through the magic of leverage, which is produced by using margin deposits, as discussed in Chapter Two. Since it is next to impossible to consistently make the right decision in commodity trading, the important thing is to cut losses, and walk away from bad trades with no remorse.

But commodity trading has other advantages besides the ability to make large profits with a small investment. Trading in commodities offers a level of liquidity that it not available in any other investment. If you buy stocks, bonds, real estate, or any other appreciating asset, including art or jewelry, your capital is tied up in that asset. When you trade in the futures markets, your margin balances continue to be available to you, as long as you cover any of the losses that have occurred on your account. If you have profits in your trading account, you can take them out without liquidating your position; if you have a profit on any other investment such as stocks, bonds, or real estate, you have to sell the asset in order to realize your profit.

Another advantage is the relative compactness of the commodity market. There are literally tens of thousands of stocks and mutual funds to invest in and an unlimited range of tangible assets (such as real estate and art) to choose from; there are only about forty futures markets that are actively traded. Nevertheless, these futures markets offer a full diversity of market segments so that the trader can trade on whatever economic forces he deems to be pushing markets at any given time. And the trader can make money whether he thinks the market is going up or down; although you can also sell stocks short, most other investments do not offer the flexibility of "shorting" the market in this way. You cannot sell real estate or a work of art that you do not own, for example. In this way, commodity traders can make money in down markets when people who are holding stocks and bonds are losing. All of these advantages must, however, be balanced against the inherent risk of commodities.

COMMODITIES BENEFIT FROM INFLATION

Most assets (except perhaps real estate) do not benefit from rising inflation, particularly unexpected inflation, but commodities usually do. Increased demand for goods and services pushes up the price of those goods and services and therefore the price of the commodities used to produce those goods and services. Because of this phenomenon, commodity prices are usually rising when inflation is accelerating, and investing in commodities may prove an ideal hedge against inflation in one's portfolio. Any trader who feels we are entering an inflationary period would feel compelled to hold a long position in commodities. Because of the ability to go short, traders can also play on recessionary or deflationary trends and hold short positions in commodity futures.

Commodity prices had their ups and downs during the 1980s and 1990s, but ended the period at roughly the same level where they began. This was due to a number of factors. For one, there was less demand for commodities as a hedge against inflation, since inflation was mostly falling during this period. Also, consumer spending in the United States, which dominated global demand during the period, moved drastically away from manufacturing and toward the service sector, which requires fewer commodities to produce than manufactured goods. Commodities and financial assets react differently to rising inflation, particularly if it is unexpected. This is another reason that holding commodities in a portfolio is beneficial. For instance, a higher rate of inflation could raise interest rates and therefore the cost for corporations to borrow, which will have an adverse effect on both stocks and bonds, while it increases the demand for commodities as a hedge against inflation. This would bring a portfolio into balance in terms of exposure to inflation.

Stocks and bonds tend to perform better when the inflation rate is stable or even slowing. This is because increased inflation lowers the value of future cash flows of the companies represented by the stocks and bonds. These future dollars are not able to buy as many goods and services as they would today. For example, the bull markets in stocks and bonds during the 1980s and 1990s occurred primarily because of the fall in the rate of inflation. This phenomenon is changing, as emerging nations are pushing up the demand for raw materials. China alone, with 1.3 billion people, is consuming more foodstuffs, using more fuel, and building more homes and factories.

Factors in other investment markets are also undergoing change. Stock prices appear overpriced on an historic basis. The elemental measurement of the value of a stock, the P/E (price/earnings) ratio is currently at extreme highs on the NASDAQ in comparison to past markets. Can the equity market continue to support these inflated prices? Current low-interest rates make the bond market a very uninteresting alternative to either stocks or commodities. Yields on government bonds are extremely low and good corporate bonds with better yields are extremely expensive. Real estate market values seem also to have topped out, and prices that have been rising in the double digits from the mid 1990s are flattening and even falling in some locations.

Another factor to consider is that inflation occurs in periods of rapid economic growth, creating a rising demand for the goods and services created from commodities. This higher demand for finished goods and services boosts the price of commodities, especially if this demand increases in developing regions of the world. If the segment of the world that is considering "growing" is itself growing, we can continue to expect unforeseen pressure on demand for raw materials as well as consumer goods. (We will see later how the demand for consumer goods fuels the demand, and the prices, of commodities.)

Commodity prices are not necessarily contingent upon the health of the economy. According to Jim Rogers in Hot Commodities, "The longest bull market in commodities began during the Great Depression in 1933 and grew even stronger during that period, and thirty years later, during the famous world wide recession of the 1970s, commodity prices skyrocketed again."

Commodities may also react differently to other changes in economic or market conditions than stocks and bonds. For example, if the OPEC nations unexpectedly decide to reduce the supply of oil by a significant amount, the price of oil, gasoline, and heating oil would likely rise. (The basic concept of supply and demand at work.) Natural gas prices might rise as well if industrial consumers switched from oil to gas. These rising energy costs could lead to higher commodity prices in general. This would negatively impact corporations' bottom lines, since their total costs of business would rise significantly. This would affect the prices of both stocks and bonds. We continually see this domino effect where rising prices of raw materials force down the profits of companies, while the prices of commodities, the bases of those raw materials, increase, further pushing raw materials costs for firms, and further reducing profitability.

Note that the oil crises of the 1970s and 1980s were associated with major recessions at the time. Examples include the Arab OPEC oil embargo associated with the Yom Kippur War of 1973, and the oil price increase shocks of 1979-1980 and 1990-1991. Oil shocks disrupt economic activity since unexpected increases in oil prices usually lead to declines in the economy, as measured by both output and employment. (Ironically, major falls in oil prices can precipitate economic crises as well, as the oil price collapse of 1986 proved. Steady and escalating oil prices led to an increase in capacity and an overconfidence in the energy sector led banks to overextend themselves in this supposedly robust area of the economy. This was especially true in the Savings and Loan industry, since a series of changes in federal and state laws had allowed S&Ls to invest outside their traditional business areas. Many of the loans and lines of credit could grow with escalating oil prices since they were collateralized by increasingly more valuable inventory. Some became dependent on these continued high energy prices. When the Saudis flooded the world market with oil as a reaction to quota violations of the other OPEC nations, the price of oil collapsed, and with it, oil refineries and their banks.)

Commodities may also provide a hedge against other "event risks," a catchall phrase meaning the risk of financial crisis, war or other political events that may cause other assets to fall. The demand for raw materials typically rises in these events, and the raw commodity is seen as a safer haven than the corporate world. Some commodities, precious metals, for example, are frequently viewed as safe havens from all financial and political risk. The fact that commodity returns are "negatively correlated" with another asset class, such as stocks, does not mean that commodity prices always fall when stock prices are rising; it means that commodity returns will probably be lower than their long-term averages when stocks are yielding returns higher than their long-term average.

Aside from these compelling arguments, one of the main reasons to invest in commodities is diversification. Commodities are a distinct asset class with returns that are largely independent of stock and bond returns. Therefore, adding broad commodity exposure can help diversify a portfolio of stocks and bonds, lowering risk and potentially boosting return. Achieving this diversification has been made easier with the development of investment products that passively track a broad range of commodities.

Why then, despite the potential diversification benefits of commodities, do most investors stick to financial assets in their portfolios? Stocks and bonds have traditionally been easier to invest in and commodities have been known as volatile. However, the recent development of products that make investing in commodity futures easier for investors should allow them to reap the benefits from diversification that commodities provide. In this way, volatility in commodities can actually be a positive factor in formulating an overall portfolio strategy.

This does not mean that an investor can add some commodities to his portfolio and then forget about them, any more than the investor would do this with his portfolio of stocks and bonds. Active management and knowledge application is required in either case. Whether an investor chooses to engage in this management himself, or through a managed account, the skills of the manager have a significant effect on performance.

DEMAND FOR COMMODITIES

There is a strong demand for commodities because of the development of emerging economies, such as China and India, and also because of worldwide surging demand for oil in the face of diminishing supplies. The world today is clambering for resources, and the world of prices is legislated by the laws of supply and demand. The growing developed world as well as the emerging developing world will be scrambling and competing for resources with the developed world. This means that now may be one of the best times to enter the world of commodity trading. The shift of China and India into mainstream economies will lead to an unprecedented demand for commodities. Let us look at the growing Japanese economy in the 1950s as an example. Oil consumption by Japan grew from 1950 to 1970 from 1 barrel per person per year to more than 17 barrels per person per year. China and India consume oil at a similar early stage rate of 1 barrel per person per year. But China and India's populations are 18 times the size of Japan's. From pure extrapolation, this would mean that in 20 years, the world's stocks of oil, as well as other commodities, will not be sufficient to meet this tremendous demand. Oil is nonrenewable, so other materials will have to be found to replace it over time. This will put pressure on the prices of the current alternatives, such as ethanol or bio-diesel from corn sugar and soybeans. But the Chinese and Indians and the rest of the world are not going to stop eating. Demand for these commodities as foodstuffs will compete with demand for them as energy sources. Even if the Chinese and Indians wanted to become more self-sufficient in food products, they would continue to consume important commodities such as potash to fertilize their fields, and their growing middle classes will demand automobiles and computers, which will use such other basic commodities as aluminum, lead, gold, and platinum. This will push industrialization of these economies, further fueling this demand. This anticipated increase in total global commodity consumption is probably one of the strongest arguments for including commodities in a portfolio.

SUMMARY

Let us recapitulate the benefits of commodities trading.

Over the last 43 years, the average annualized return to an investment in commodity futures has been comparable to the return on the S&P 500, and both outperformed corporate bonds.

Commodity futures outperformed stocks in the 1970s. This trend was reversed during the 1990s, but overall, the average return has been comparable. In other words, commodities perform as well as stocks and frequently much better.

Investors are ultimately concerned with the real purchasing power of their returns, which means that inflation is a major concern for investors, since it erodes the underlying value of the asset, even as its nominal value in increasing. Most traditional asset classes such as bank deposits and stocks and bonds are a poor hedge against inflation, at least over the short and medium term, and investors should therefore seek alternatives. Earning double digit rates on a CD is not an attractive return when the rate of inflation is approaching 15 %, as we witnessed in the early 1980s. Even though bond yields are set to compensate investors for expected inflation over the life of the bond, when inflation turns out to be higher than the level investors contracted for (when they bought the bonds), the real purchasing power of the cash flows falls short of expectations, and the nominal value of the bonds is lower.

Equities (stocks) should provide a better hedge than bonds against inflation, at least in theory. Since stocks represent claims against the real assets of companies (factories, equipment, inventories, etc.) whose value can be expected to hold pace with the general price level, the price of the corporation that the assets belong to should also keep pace. However, firms also have contracts with suppliers of inputs and have labor and capital costs that are fixed in nominal terms and therefore increase in price with the increase in value of assets. Inflation is associated with a negative impact on total corporate output, which usually means bad news for the equities markets. Experience has shown that stocks do not provide much of a hedge against inflation.

Commodity futures make a much better inflation hedge than stocks or bonds because commodity futures represent the risk of commodity prices, which are directly linked to the components of inflation. In addition, since commodity futures prices include all available market information about trends in commodity prices, they will rise and fall even if the deviations from inflation trends are completely unexpected. This is why commodity futures do well when stocks and bonds perform poorly. In other words, stocks and bonds are negatively correlated with inflation, while commodity futures are positively correlated. These kinds of inflation correlations tend to increase with the holding period, so that the longer you hold commodity positions as compared to positions in stocks and bonds, the more the inflation protection will accrue.

We have seen that commodity futures are useful in creating diversified portfolios with respect to outright returns. But there is also evidence of another important diversification effect, and that is a timing effect. Commodity futures perform well in the early stages of a recession, a time when stock returns are generally poor. In later stages of recessions, commodity returns fall off, usually when equities are gaining. This deviation from the business cycle of equities provides a further level of protection from longer term cyclical swings.

4

HOW TO GET INTO COMMODITY TRADING

"Selling a soybean contract short is worth two years at the Harvard Business School."

— Robert Stovall, Managing Director,
Wood Asset Management

To trade in commodity futures, one has to open an account with a futures broker, someone who is licensed to conduct business on behalf of clients at the Exchange. This doesn't sound too daunting, and most people who are at this stage of the investment journey have probably already opened accounts for stock trading accounts, mutual funds accounts, or IRAs. In addition, banks and brokerage companies are making it easy for investors to spread their risks by dealing in many different types of markets. Banks offering traditional banking services now realize the potential of offering commodity brokerage services to their clients as well. In 2007, JPMorgan Chase & Co., the third-largest U.S. bank, announced that it was going to increase its global commodity trading staff by more than 30 percent within a year to exploit the boom in raw materials prices and help clients protect against swings in energy and metal prices. The bank intends to add 40 people to the 110 in commodity trading and marketing, said Catherine Flax, co-head of JPMorgan's global energy business. She also noted that the biggest expansion is in energy. UBS AG and Lehman Brothers Holdings Inc. are among other banks that have expanded into commodity trading as they see the prices for oil, copper, and other raw materials rising to record levels. Commodity trading is coming to the everyman when these giant financial institutions expand operations to include a broader swathe of the investing public in their expansion plans.

You will need to have to have a separate brokerage account for your commodity trading. It would be very convenient if you could use your regular stock brokerage account to trade futures as well, but that is not how the market is organized. Each of these segments of investments is controlled by different regularity authorities. The Commodity Futures Trading Commission (CFTC) regulates commodities brokerages and the Securities and Exchange Commission (SEC) regulates stock brokerages.

There are many ways you can start trading in commodities. You can do your own research and make independent decisions, or you can hire an advisor who does the research and gives you recommendations. Engaging a Commodities Trading Advisor, or CTA, requires paying a fee that cuts into your overall return. Nevertheless, it is advisable for new traders to work with a full-service broker, at least until they learn the ropes, as we discuss below. Bear in mind that working with a full-service broker does not guarantee top service. This is another area where it is important to do your own research and make sure the firm has a good reputation.

All firms and brokers are registered with the National Futures Association, and this organization lists firms that have had violations with the NFA or the CFTC, just as the Better Business Bureau lists claims against businesses. Be sure to research your potential broker with the NFA to make sure you are working with a reputable broker who cares about his customers. Some disgruntled customers are inevitable, but if a brokerage firm has an excessive number of claims you should steer clear of it.

You can also invest through a managed futures account or fund. Managed futures accounts have outperformed the S&P 500 by more than 35% over the past year, but like the standard disclaimers always announce, past success is not guarantee of future performance. Part of recent success is nothing more than a function of the stock market's decline—in falling markets, investors protect or "hedge" their cash investments by buying insurance in the form of a futures contract. An investor can buy the right to sell the corresponding number of futures contracts that equal his or her cash position to maintain the status quo, or alter the number of contracts to increase return. The drawback to managed futures is their volatility, and the inability to respond quickly to dramatic market movements.

Futures funds are offered through financial advisors such as CTAs, as well as through brokerages. These funds are set up as limited partnerships, meaning your losses cannot exceed your original investment. And by investing in a diverse basket of commodities, some funds have been able to minimize volatility. Managed futures funds are similar to hedge funds with lock-up periods and windows for quarterly withdrawals. You must pass a suitability requirement and meet the minimum (usually $10,000) investment requirement.

Another alternate way to invest in commodities is to invest in a commodity index fund. Investment vehicles that track commodity futures indices are not the same as actively managed futures accounts. Instead, commodity index returns provide passive exposure to a broad range of commodities. For example, the Dow Jones AIG Commodity Index tracks the futures price of 20 different commodities, including energy, livestock, grains, industrial metals, precious metals, and "soft" commodities. Changes to the composition of the index are determined by preset rules rather than a manager's discretion. These rules may include switching from a commodity that has had continuous adverse trading conditions in a single contract, or major changes in the global consumption pattern. As is the case with the composition of the Dow Jones Industrial Average that most investors are familiar with for stocks, these compositions are infrequently adjusted (usually not more than once a year) so that the index maintains a consistent link to the commodities.

One advantage of commodity exposure that tracks a broad index is that commodities are not highly correlated with each other and index returns should be less volatile than the returns on an individual commodity. Another advantage is that commodity indexes themselves have existed for decades, providing ample historic data for asset allocation studies and research.

HOW TO FIND A BROKER

Let's first understand what a broker is. A commodities broker is the person who buys and sells commodities on behalf of others (clients). For this service, he is paid a fee or commission which is usually fixed by the regulatory board of an Exchange. He many be attached to a brokerage house, an investment bank, an exchange or a clearing house. Commodities brokers earn their commissions whether the client gains or loses money. This is an important fact to consider, since commissions are earned on trades, and the more trades (winning OR losing trades) that a broker makes on behalf of a client, the more he will make. Many commodities brokers operate their own firms, which means that they are not only placing orders for their clients, but are also managing their own speculative trading positions.

Commodity brokers are located in most cities. You can find a good futures broker through referrals, and of course, you can also find thousands of online commodity brokers. There are several types of brokerage firms. You can choose a full-service brokerage if you want to be able to trade in several markets. In these, you work out your trading strategy in close cooperation with your broker. Full-service brokers are advisable for those who are new to futures or commodity trading. They offer great advice and can provide a wealth of data. A good full-service brokerage firm keeps you updated on the latest happenings in the markets. With this kind of frequent interaction, a customer usually feels more secure that his money is being invested in the right place and commodity. Of course, a full-service broker will cost you more because of the number of value-added services they provide.

There are also many online discount brokerage firms to choose from. These discount brokerage firms allow the client to make all the decisions about his trading account. All the customer does is call them, place an order, and the online discount brokerage firm picks up the order and executes it. If you are interested in doing your own research on the various commodities, discount brokerage firms are ideal to work with. The disadvantage is that, unlike full-service brokerage firms, they do not offer additional services. Discount brokerages are a good option once you have become confident in your trading abilities.

Another type of broker is an online introducing broker, who specializes in futures trading through a well-known established firm. These brokers offer the same services as a full-service firm and are spread across the country, usually in smaller cities.

Interview a number of brokers before you commit to one. Choosing a futures broker is a personal decision, like choosing a stockbroker, dentist, or lawyer. Most large brokerage houses that deal with stocks and bonds also have divisions that trade commodities, and now many banks are offering services in commodity trading. If an investor is generally happy with the relationship and performance of the brokerage, expanding the range of investments to commodities will be fairly easy and straightforward.

In addition, many Exchanges have a service that recommends brokers. Whichever method you use, be clear about expectations on both sides. Make a list of questions and ensure that this person is someone you will be comfortable working with. This is a two way street, and a broker should clearly understand the client's goals, needs and level of expertise. In other words, does the client have strong ideas of his own or does he want and need a lot of help and advice? On the other hand, any prospective client should endeavor to obtain as much information as possible about the broker and his trading philosophy, as well as track record. Of course, the client will have to take the word of a broker as to his track record. Since accounts are held in the name of clients, it is the client's account that is successful or not, and that is not information that can be tracked. This is one of the reasons it is advisable to rely on referrals rather than shopping around. A client should be wary of a broker who is vague about the success of his other clients' portfolios or does not ask important questions about the client's investment goals and is not willing to have frank discussions about how their trading concepts and goals fit in with the client's. Beware any broker who just wants to "get you in the door" without understanding each of his client's ultimate goals.

A potential trader in commodities futures should clearly understand the financial requirements involved. If a broker does not explain these requirements thoroughly, let the buyer beware. A broker who plays down the costs and initial financial outlay is only interested in some quick commissions before he moves onto his next prey. If the broker does not seriously analyze the client's ability to operate in this market, he is not interested in the long term success of the client's investments. Also beware of brokers who overly hype the market without any disclaimers as to the risks involved. Yes, commodity trading can be very lucrative, but there are few overnight successes and even fewer constant successes.

A client should only work with a broker who is very clear about the risks instead of painting a rosy picture of a market where the client cannot lose.

There is no certification process for broker/analysts, as there might be for a CPA (Certified Public Accountant) or a CFA (Certified Financial Analyst), although they must be licensed by and registered with the NFA. Brokers don't necessarily have to have any specialized training to practice as a broker, but they will usually have a college degree. Since they must be familiar with economic fundamentals and trends, most brokers will have a degree in finance or economics, although a successful sales background is probably one of the most common qualifications. Commodity brokers must fulfill state licensing requirements, which means passing a licensing test. Only work with a broker who is registered with one of the regulatory agencies such as the CFTC or the NFA. (If you choose to work through a "managed account," your broker will have to be registered and have passed a certification process — see below.) Make sure your broker trades through a regulated commodity exchange. Obtain and read all of the literature explaining how transactions are conducted and the risks you are taking. Understand and agree to, ahead of time, the fee schedule and margin policy. Ask how long the broker has been in business and how long he has been with this firm. Learn as much as you can about the firm and its partners; they can be almost as much as a risk to you as the broker you work with. You may want to choose a broker who has relationships with brokers of every major exchange in Chicago and New York, so that you are not limited in the choice of commodities you can trade in over time.

TYPES OF ACCOUNTS

Once you have found a broker to work with, you have to decide on the kind of account you want. Discuss these options before choosing a brokerage, since brokerage houses may have their own definitions and features.

A self-directed, or non-discretionary individual account, means that the client makes all of the trading decisions. If a client feels he has mastered the fundamentals of commodities and of the markets, he will want to make these decisions. This does not differentiate from a full service brokerage account; the client still makes the decisions with a full service broker, but the broker gives him guidance. Many times, the brokerage firm has a capital requirement and requires that you have a minimum investment in the account. The commission scale may be different for self-directed accounts and there may be maintenance fees in addition, so understand all of the fees ahead of time.

In a managed account, the concept is more like "leave the driving to us." The responsibility of making all of the trades is taken over by the broker. This may be the ideal solution for an investor who wants to be in commodities, but does not want to spend time doing the necessary research and following the markets on a daily basis. In the case of a managed account, the client discusses his goals and risk tolerance with the broker, and the broker and client design an investment strategy together. A Commodity Trading Advisor (CTA) is the professional at a brokerage firm who manages the account. This kind of an advisor is licensed by the National Association of Securities Dealers as well as the National Futures Association to "offer advice on commodities and to accept compensation for investment and management services." Like a registered stockbroker who has to pass the Series 7, the CTA must pass an exam called the Series 3 that tests financial, trading, and portfolio management knowledge. And like a stockbroker, the commodity broker has his own management and investment ideas and the client should make sure they are in line with his own.

Just as mutual funds exist to allow investors the benefit of investing in the stock market without the worry and concentrated risk of holding individual stocks, commodity pools exist for commodity investors to achieve the same end. Though true mutual funds in commodities do not exist (but may be on their way — some hybrid funds exist such as the PIMCO CommodityRealReturn Strategy Fund), a commodity pool, usually organized as a limited partnership, combines the capital of a number of investors to invest in commodities.

Another way to be involved without buying and selling contracts is to buy shares of a Master Limited Partnership that specializes in the production, transformation, and distribution of commodities. An MLP issues shares, called units, and these units are traded on the public exchanges such as the New York Stock Exchange and the NASDAQ. An investment in an MLP is an investment in a public partnership with operations exposed to the rewards and risks of commodities, but without direct trading. There are also some tax advantages to being a unit holder in an MLP, which are beyond the scope of this book.

WHAT IT COSTS TO HAVE AN ACCOUNT

Services

A trader should subscribe to a quote service in order to watch the action. There are a lot of quote services, with a wide range in prices for the service. Get a recommendation from your broker. You can probably subscribe to a "delayed" quote system, where the price quotes are 20-40 minutes behind the actual trade, or for free from some of the Exchanges or news services. Live quotes, of course, are not free, but such a system may be necessary if you have decided to work without a broker and need to see where the market is trading at any given moment.

Quote services also offer charting capabilities, news bulletins, and other services for the commodity you are interested in. If you work with a broker, you may be able to receive these services as part of your brokerage fee. The cost of subscribing to quoting and charting services should play a role in a client's decision about working with a full service broker. Subscribing to a number of services may prove to be more costly than a brokerage fee that bundles all of these services and also supplies market advice. If you want to avail yourself of additional services, choose one or two and get used to using and interpreting them before you add any others. For those who are willing to do additional research, there is a great deal of information available on the Web that can be accessed for free, so it is advisable to use as much of that as possible before paying for additional services.

Commissions

In commodities, commissions are charged per contract. This may feel like sticker shock to someone used to trading in equities where there is a flat commission based on a number of shares. It would not be unusual to buy 1,000 shares of stock and pay a commission of only $20, whereas if you buy 2 contracts, you may pay a $100 commission. But when you buy the stocks, you are paying the full price of the stock; when you buy a futures contract, you only have to lay out the amount of the margin, so you control a much greater dollar value of a good.

Margins

Margins serve as a performance bond that protects you, your brokerage firm, and the entire exchange. If the balance in your margin account falls to a level that does not absorb potential loss, you have to increase your margin. Make sure you understand the margin policy of both the exchange you are trading on and of the brokerage serving your account so there are no nasty surprises. Margin requirements vary according to the commodity traded, so if you have limited funds to invest, your choice of commodities will be limited.

One of the key things to consider when you are trading commodities is keeping your costs down. Especially for a small trader, where each trade is only capable of yielding a small profit, having too many fees and other costs can quickly erode what little profit the trader may be able to generate.

TRADING STRATEGIES

You pick up the phone and call the broker, or go online and enter an order — and you are trading. Pretty simple? It can be, but the money in the margin account would be gone quickly if a trader just decided to start trading without any understanding of the markets and the strategies used in the markets.

Even if you decide to participate in futures trading in a way that does not involve day-to-day trading decisions (such as a managed account or commodity pool), it is nonetheless useful to understand the dollars and cents of how futures trading gains and losses are realized. And, of course, if you intend to trade your own account, such an understanding is essential.

Dozens of different strategies and variations of strategies are employed by futures traders in pursuit of speculative profits. Here is a brief description and illustration of several basic strategies.

Buying (Going Long) to Profit From an Expected Price Increase

Someone expecting the price of a particular commodity to increase over a given period of time can seek to profit by buying futures contracts. If the trader is correct in forecasting the direction and timing of the price change, the futures contract can later be sold for the higher price, thereby yielding a profit. If the price declines rather than increases, the trade results in a loss. Because of leverage, the gain or loss may be greater than the initial margin deposit.

For example, assume it is now June and the December Corn contract is presently quoted at 405.40, and over the coming months you expect the price to increase. You decide to deposit the required margins of $2,350 per contract and buy 100 December Corn. Further assume that by September, the December Corn futures price has risen to 415.4 and you decide to take your profit by selling. Since each contract is for 5,000 bushels, your 10-cent a bushel profit on your 100 contracts would be 5,000 bushels x 10 cents x 100 or $50,000 less transaction costs. Don't forget, through the miracle of leverage, you controlled this $2,027,000 position in corn until it reached $2,077,000 with your margin deposit of only $235,000. But, lucky you, since the market went the way you thought it would, your margin deposit earned you $50,000 (more than 21% in 3 months), or an annualized return of 85%.

Suppose, however, that rather than rising to 415.40, the December Corn futures price had declined to 395.40 and that, in order to avoid the possibility of further loss, you elect to sell the contract at that price. On 100 contracts, the 10-cent a bushel change would now mean a loss of $50,000 plus transaction costs. In other words, on an "investment" of $235,000 (which would have increased due to margin calls as the price declined; your broker would have been calling you, as needed, for additional margin funds to cover the loss), you would have lost $50,000, or more than 21%. It is unlikely that a trader would let a loss run for that long, so this is an extreme example of the power (both positive and negative) of leveraging.

Selling (Going Short) to Profit From an Expected Price Decrease

Instead of first buying a futures contract, you first sell a futures contract. If, as expected, the price declines, a profit can be realized by later purchasing an offsetting futures contract at the lower price. The gain per unit will be the amount by which the purchase price is below the earlier selling price. For traders of the physical commodity, this short sell on the futures market works to hedge their exposure in the physical market.

For example, in June a farmer expects to harvest at least 10,000 bushels of beans during September. By hedging, he can lock in a price for his soybeans and protect himself against the possibility of falling prices.

At the time, the cash price for new-crop soybeans is $6 and the price of November bean futures is $6.25. The delivery month of November marks the harvest of new-crop soybeans. The farmer would "short" hedge his crop by selling two November 5,000 bushel soybean futures contracts at $6.25. (Once again we are using a simplistic approach, since, typically, farmers do not hedge 100 percent of their expected production, as the exact number of bushels produced is unknown until harvest. In this scenario, the producer expects to produce more than 10,000 bushels of soybeans. In addition, the concepts of bid/ask and the price of commissions are omitted.)

By the beginning of September, cash and futures prices have fallen. When the farmer sells his cash beans to the local elevator for $5.72 a bushel, he lifts his hedge by purchasing November soybean futures at $5.95. The 30-cent gain in the futures market offsets the lower price he receives for his soybeans to the cash market. For the farmer, if the market goes the other way, he will sell his cash crop at a higher price and lose money in the futures market. But that was the price of the "insurance policy" (the hedge) that he was willing to pay in order to avoid the risk of falling prices. For farmers, the gamble is removed by using such a hedge.

As we have learned, however, speculative traders such as you have now become are in the business of taking on such gambles. There is no physical commodity that they own and need to protect against falling prices. Research may indicate that there may be money to be made in falling commodity prices. For example, assume that in June, available information indicates a probable decrease in cattle prices over the next several months. In the hopes of profiting, you deposit an initial margin of $2,000 and sell one December live cattle futures contract at a price of 94.40 (94.4 cents per pound). Each contract is for 40,000 pounds, meaning each 1-cent per pound change in price will increase or decrease the value of the futures contract by $400. If, by September, the price has declined to 89.40 (.894 cents a pound), an offsetting futures contract would be purchased at 5 cents a pound below the original selling price. On the 40,000-pound contract, that is a gain of 5 cents x 40,000 pounds, or buying back the contract at $2,000 less than was paid.

Let us assume once again that you were wrong. Instead of decreasing, the December live cattle futures price increases to .9940 cents a pound by the time you decide to liquidate your short futures position through an offsetting purchase. The outcome would then be a loss of 5 cents a pound on the futures transaction resulting in a loss of $2,000, since the contract had to be bought back at a higher price than it was sold at. It would also result in the total loss of the $2,000 which was deposited as initial margin, plus any transaction costs.

The difference in the soybean versus the live cattle examples is that the hedger, such as the farmer, is not looking to make money off of the futures market, but only to protect himself in the physicals market. The hedger has an offsetting asset that will increase or decrease in value against the futures contract. The investor is risking his money, with no offsetting asset, and so will have a pure gain or loss on the futures trade.

Basis

Another concept that influences both the market and the amount of money a hedger gains or loses is the basis. Differentials between the cash price and the futures price are called the basis. If a short hedger has a widening of the basis (the cash price has fallen to a point greater than the futures price), a basis loss may result. The short hedger's cash position loss may be greater than the gain realized on the futures side of the transaction. Of course, a basis gain will occur with a widening basis on a long hedge. The futures would rise in price to a greater degree than the cash price.

Spreads

The objective behind a spread is not to make money on the rise or fall in the price of a commodity, but to make money from a change in the relationship between different prices. When a trader "puts on" a spread, he will buy one contract and simultaneously sell another. His position is then long and short at the same time, but in either two related commodities (soybeans and soybean meal, an intermarket spread) or two different months of the same commodity (July Corn and September Corn, an intramarket spread). The relative change between the two will determine his gain or loss. The idea is that even though spreads tend to move in the same direction, sometimes they do not, or sometimes they move at different speeds. Margins are less for spreads because they are generally less risky, but the ability to profit in both an up or down situation is the main advantage of spread trading. There are some "traditional" spreads that are popular such as the new crop/old crop spread in many agricultural commodities, the hog/cattle spread, or one of the most popular, the "crack spread", the spread between heating oil and unleaded gasoline or other refined products, caused by seasonal variations that push the prices of these commodities toward or away from each other. (Cracking the crude is the expression used to indicate that it is refined.) Spreads are also referred to as straddles or switches.

REGULATIONS

Regulations that apply to stock and bond markets do not apply to commodities. In the United States, the Commodities Futures Trading Commission (CFTC), an agency of the U.S. Department of Agriculture, oversees exchange traded futures and options (much as the SEC regulates stocks), the exchanges they are traded on, and the brokerage firms, money managers, and commodity advisors who deal in them. The first level of regulation for commodity trading is the exchange that the commodity is traded on. The exchange safeguards against counterparty credit risk and default, assures that margin requirements and trading and delivery procedures are followed and enforces regulations by fines and suspensions. Members of exchanges must meet financial solvency standards. For example, a clearing member of the NYMEX must show a minimum working capital of $2 million and make a deposit of 10% of the firm's capital into the exchange's guarantee fund. In other words, the financial strength of the Exchange is based upon the combined financial strength of all of its members. In addition to the CFTC, the National Futures Association (NFA), which is a self-regulatory body, oversees the activities of its members. Over the Counter (OTC) or non-exchange markets do not offer these guarantees and do not fall under any governmental regulatory body. They are only therefore regulated through normal business law.

Even though there are regulations for commodity trading, some things that cannot be done in the stock market can be done in the commodities markets. For example, there are no bans on insider trading. In the commodity markets, anyone can say just about anything they want about the market, they can float rumors, etc. The trader has to decide which information to accept, and which to discard.

Firms and individuals that conduct futures trading business

with the public are subject to regulation by the CFTC and NFA. NFA is a congressionally authorized self-regulatory organization subject to CFTC oversight. Firms and individuals that violate NFA rules of professional ethics and conduct, or that fail to comply with strictly enforced financial and record-keeping requirements can, if circumstances warrant, be permanently barred from engaging in any futures-related business with the public. The enforcement powers of the CFTC are similar to those of other major federal regulatory agencies, including the power to seek criminal prosecution by the Department of Justice where circumstances warrant such action.

5

FUNDAMENTAL ANALYSIS

"The fundamental things apply, as time goes by."

— *Herman Hupfeld*

Another important concept in trading commodities is "fundamentals" versus "technicals." Fundamental analysis refers to studying the basics that influence the price of a commodity: supply and demand, of course, but also weather, social trends, and the general economy. Technical analysis refers to charting prices and looking for certain movements that confirm or predict a continuation or reversal in a given trend. Technical analysts contend that the commercial users of commodity futures are the most active traders, and therefore their activity, and the prices reflecting their activity, are the most accurate indicators of the demand elasticity of the market. Most traders use a combination of the two types of analysis, since they feel that more information they have, the better decisions they can make. Fundamental analysis examines the market's environment and technical data examines the market's data.

Some commodities rely more heavily than others on any one given type of analysis. Oils tend to rely more on fundamentals while financials tend to rely more on technical charts.

Other principles to consider in futures trading are "backwardation" and "contango." Backwardation is a condition in which forward prices are lower than spot prices; contango is when forward prices are higher than spot prices. They are fundamental indicators since they are based on basic price theories; since they fit many technical data analyses they will be addressed in more detail in the Chapter on technical analysis.

One of the most basic fundamentals was already discussed in Chapter Three: supply and demand. Price theory of economics dictates that the price of any given good will settle at a point where the demand and supply for it meet, or are at equilibrium. All fundamentals of commodity trading feed off this one. In agricultural commodities, the crop and weather reports impact the markets because they impact the supply of the commodity. In the oil markets, inventory and political upheaval strongly impact prices because of their effect on supply. The metals markets are heavily influenced by interest rates because of the carry costs of that commodity. In the financial and foreign exchange markets, interest rates as well as government policy create more or less demand for the financial instrument or currency. And of course, the fundamentals move across commodity lines, since weather can influence the price of oil, and carry costs also affect agricultural commodities, and interest rates affect everything. There are literally hundreds of supply and demand factors influencing commodity futures at any one time.

A few basic tenets apply. Each commodity has its own set of fundamentals that will affect it. Some fundamentals affect all commodities; some fundamentals will affect certain commodities more than others. In addition, there are probably almost as many fundamentals to examine as there are analysts examining them, and some of the data may be useless information. But there are basics to understand and to follow.

SUPPLY AND DEMAND

Economics 101 taught us that if supply remains constant and demand increases, prices will increase and that if demand remains constant and supplies increase, prices will decrease. This adjustment continues until the price where supply equals demand and equilibrium is found. It is simple in principle but not so simple in practice, since this "dance" between supply and demand never stops and therefore prices constantly change.

The supply of a given commodity is not easily increased, since it frequently requires investment in the infrastructure of an industry, such as new mines or oilfields, or at least a shifting of resources, such as corn to soybeans. These demands are ever increasing in recent years, and it is not just emerging societies that are creating this increasing demand. Americans are building bigger and bigger homes, which require more and more heat and electricity, and driving bigger and bigger cars, which require more oil. And these new "necessities" require more and more lumber, steel, aluminum, and other raw materials. Investors must predict how supply and demand will impact future value, and which reports and statistics have historically shown a bias, thus anticipating changes ahead of the market.

WEATHER

Weather is intricately entwined with the supply and demand of most commodities. A warm winter can create excess supplies of oil and natural gas. Weather-related risks that affect commodity production can be as or more important than commodity price risks, and weather events are an unending source of problems for agricultural producers. While severe weather and weather events affect all countries, they more severely and disproportionately impact developing countries and their agricultural production, which represent a major segment of the commodities markets (for example, coffee and cocoa in African regions and soybeans and orange juice in South America). Although farmers try to mitigate weather risk as much as possible through practices such as irrigation and conservation tillage, which protect soil and add moisture, these activities are not sufficient to protect against major weather-related price swings.

Weather has such an enormous impact on commodities that commodity traders and analysts pay hundreds and even thousands of dollars a month for newsletters, commentaries, and other services that attempt to make long-range weather forecasts. The guiding median for traders in the agricultural commodities is an elusive concept called normal weather. For example, if the forecast for summer rainfall for the corn belt in Nebraska, Iowa, and Illinois is for above-normal precipitation, corn futures may rise in anticipation of the crop getting too much moisture, which would stunt its growth. However, the same principle would apply if the forecast was for too little rainfall, since yields would be lower. If the forecast calls for near normal rainfall, invariably the price of corn will fall in anticipation of a very good crop and too many bushels of corn on the market in the fall and winter. As in all of the fundamental, and even technical factors affecting commodity futures prices, other influences also hold sway; a perfect rain scenario during the growing season should mean lower prices, but recent competition for corn as an alternative fuel source may act as a counterbalance.

Not just agricultural and soft commodities are affected by weather patterns. The price of plywood soars when tropical storms and hurricanes approach the coast of the United States. The residents in the path of these storms buy up plywood to board up windows and protect their houses, creating local shortages. These local shortages are filled by drawing on stock supplies from the rest of the country, driving up prices.

POLITICS

Geopolitical forces can play an important role in the prices of commodities. Political unrest in major oil producers such as Iran or Venezuela can have traders watching for higher prices in any of the energy products. Government protectionist agricultural programs, such as price support programs and export enhancement programs encourage farmers to plant less or more acreage of certain crops, affecting supply and consequently price. Other industries that base themselves on commodities, such as the steel industry have also experienced strong interventionist moves by politicians.

INTEREST RATES

Interest rates have an all-pervasive influence on commodities, since they are the "cost" of a commodity (money) used to purchase all other commodities. As such, interest rates affect every aspect of an economy since they control the supply and demand of one of the regulating commodities, money. They affect not only the ability of traders to invest, but also the supply of money in the markets. The Federal Reserve Bank implements economic and monetary policies that are intended to promote the smooth running of our economy (whether they do or not can be a matter of debate). By setting these policies, it has a profound effect upon interest rates and the money supply, which, in turn, dictate the rate of growth of the economy, and therefore its demand for consumer goods (products based on commodities and the commodities themselves). It is important to know and understand what the "Fed" is doing at any time.

In addition, the "carry cost" of goods and commodities is strongly influenced by interest rates. Jeffrey Frankel, an economist at Harvard University (The Effect of Interest Rates on Commodity Prices) explains this theory thus: High interest rates reduce the demand for storable commodities, or increase the supply, through a variety of channels:

- They increase the incentive for extraction today rather than tomorrow (think of the rates at which oil is pumped, forests logged, or livestock herds culled).

- They decrease firms' desire to carry inventories (think of oil inventories held in tanks).

- They encourage speculators to shift out of commodity contracts (spot and forward), and into financial instruments.

All three mechanisms work to reduce the market price of commodities, as happened when real interest rates were high in the early 1980s. A decrease in real interest rates has the opposite effect, lowering the cost of carrying inventories, and raising commodity prices, as happened during 2001-2004.

INFLATION

One of the most important factors in determining the success of any investment choice is inflation. As we pointed out before, even the most risk-averse investment, a CD in an FDIC-guaranteed bank, has an inherent risk of inflation eroding not only the return on the investment but also the value of the underlying asset — money. The only asset that can actually benefit from inflation is commodities. In fact, it has been shown that the overall trend of gold tracks inflation almost perfectly:

(McClellan Financial Publications)

EMPLOYMENT NUMBERS

The "jobs report" is issued on the first Friday of each month by the U.S. Department of Labor and is closely watched by traders and investors. Since this report gives the number of people employed and unemployed, hours worked, and other key figures, it is an excellent indicator of the overall health of the economy. The health of an economy is a determining factor in the demand side of the price equation for commodities. Put simply, if people are unemployed, they cannot afford to buy anything.

RETAIL SALES

Another indicator of the health of the economy is the retail sales report which shows sales in cars, clothing, food items, electronics, building materials, etc. The numbers in this report, which are reported as a percentage change over the previous month, have a big impact on the market since traders believe that if consumers are spending less, it may indicate a slowdown in the economy or even a recession. If consumer demand slows, the demand for all commodities will also slow, since just about every commodity becomes part of an end product the consumer will ultimately use.

OTHERS

Some of the fundamentals that traders keep an eye on depend on the commodity they are active in. For example, crop reports are issued for every product grown. The numbers reported indicate the supply of the crop and, theoretically, future prices. But the other side of the supply coin is demand, and traders also have to watch trends that indicate reduction in demand. Here are other sources of information traders use.

Commitments of Traders (COT)

This report, published by the CFTC every Friday, contains general background information and detailed explanatory notes for contract markets in which twenty or more traders hold positions equal to or above certain reporting levels established by the CFTC. The Commitments of Traders report divides commodities traders into three groups: commercial traders, small speculators and large speculators. In other words, it gives the public a list of who the big players are in any given market. Many traders believe it is one of the best indicators of market direction. The report shows the long and short positions as well as changes in positions over the previous week of the different types of investors and end users, and therefore allows traders to determine from these shifts if a trend is continuing or slowing down. Individual traders watch these positions closely; if there is a majority of long positions among the commercials and the speculators, they can assume that they expect the price trend to continue upward, and their positions support it. Once we understand more about trends, we will see how valuable the Commitment of Traders Report is.

However, much of the institutional investing in some markets, such as petroleum and metals, is not included in this report because a great deal of the investing takes place in the over-the-counter or dealer market. The COT report only covers exchange-traded futures and options.

Volume and Open Interest

As discussed in Chapter Two, open interest is the total of all futures and/or option contracts entered into and not yet offset by a transaction, by delivery, or by exercise, at any given time. A contract is open when it has been entered into and not yet offset by a offsetting transaction. Volume and open interest are measurements of interest in a given commodity position. The aggregate of all long open interest is equal to the aggregate of all short open interest. The higher the open interest, the more liquid the market in that position is. Traders use the historical data to compare it to the current report to discover how liquid a given market is and what the pressures are to move the market upwards or downwards. When trade volume goes up and prices go up, there is buying pressure. When trade volume goes up and prices go down, there is increased selling pressure. Price, volume and open interest all rising simultaneously indicates a bullish market, while price, volume and open interest all declining simultaneously indicates a bearish market.

Commercials' Positions

Commercials buy and sell a lot of commodities and therefore have a lot of influence over market movements. Commercials are defined as traders who use futures contracts in that particular commodity for hedging physical positions as defined in the CFTC regulations. They are usually entities involved in the production, processing, or merchandising of a commodity and typically hold the majority of the open positions. They are the farmers, miners, processors, grain merchants, etc. with inside knowledge of conditions in the market, usually with a large capital base and strong financing structures. As such, both their activities and the perception of their activities have profound effects on how the market will move and how other traders will react to their moves.

Deliverables

The Chicago Board of Trade reports the quantities and changes in the amounts of corn, wheat, soybeans, and oats (in bushels) that are in the elevators that are licensed to deliver on the Chicago Board of Trade. These figures alert traders that there may be a squeeze if shorts are not able to find enough grain to deliver. If grains are still on the farms and not available for delivery, it can be a very bullish signal. This applies to price pressures on the nearest trading month. Deliverable commodities are differentiated from cash settled commodities. Deliverable commodities are those for which the seller has the right (but not the obligation) to make delivery of the commodity and the buyer has the right (but not the obligation) to accept delivery of the commodity. Cash settled commodities are those for which a cash settlement can be made. Feeder cattle are a cash settled commodity, for example, and the buyer and seller could settle their price differences in cash at the end of the contract period.

The United States Department of Agriculture (USDA) reports various statistics that help traders and hedgers estimate supply and demand pressure on the prices of grains. These reports supply information on:

- **Beginning stocks:** how much supply of the agricultural commodity will carry over from the previous year.

- **Production:** the crop estimate for the current year. During the growing season, the closely watched "Crop Progress Report" is issued weekly. These reports indicate how much of a given crop has been harvested at a given time. If the harvest is earlier or later than traditional or prior periods, the prices will be affected.

- **Total supply:** beginning stocks, plus production plus imports (a very small number in the case of the United States).

- **Crush:** Total amount of soybeans crushed for use as meal, oil, and other finished products.

- **Exports, seed and residual:** the USDA reports, on a weekly basis, export inspections (on Mondays) and export sales (on Thursdays), important numbers that affect supply. Seed and residual is the amount of crop held back to produce next year's crops.

- **Total demand:** the total of crush, exports, seed, and residuals.

- **Ending carryover:** total supply minus total demand equals ending stocks.

All of these reports are available to the public on the internet in PDF format which is very easy to read. Interpreting them is another matter, since historical data is necessary to calculate the changes from one period to another. Most active traders subscribe to services that offer analyses of the various statistics reported by the government.

Certain commodities are affected by the reports on fundamentals specific to that commodity. Here are some examples.

ENERGY MARKETS

Indicators that are closely watched by energy traders deal with inventories and production levels for crude oil.

One of the most popular indicators used by oil traders is the crude inventories (stock levels), which is the amount of oil currently stored for future use. The amount and fluctuation of this number gives traders an idea of the trends in production and consumption of oil over a specific period of time. This measure includes all of the U.S. crude oil and lease condensate (mixture of heavy hydrocarbons and pentanes) held at the time of the report at refineries, within pipelines and at pipeline terminals, as well as stocks held within leases.

This information is released in weekly estimates by the Energy Information Administration (EIA) every Wednesday at 10:30 a.m. EST. The American Gas Association (AGA) releases the same report on the natural gas supply on Thursdays. These numbers have an important impact on futures prices since they indicate if there is enough product to meet the demand for energy.

Energy traders compare the crude inventory number to market expectations and also to the past levels to gain insight into the future moves of the price of oil. As inventories increase over time, it is a sign that production outstrips demand, which should lead to lower energy prices. The opposite is true when inventories are decreasing.

Included in this report of inventories is a long list of additional data focused on crude oil production covering domestic production, refinery input and utilization, along with other inventory levels (motor gasoline) and import/ export data. Traders take all of this data into consideration to try and gain an idea of the fundamentals within the crude oil market. For example, traders look at refinery utilization to determine how much more capacity is available to get additional supply to the market. If refinery utilization is high, it is difficult for the refineries to increase output, which means that less supply is available to the market, and that pushes prices higher.

FEEDER CATTLE

Probably the report most closely watched by livestock traders is the "cattle on feed" report. There are three primary segments to this report: the "number of cattle on feed" category and the amount "placed on feed" category represent the number of cattle that will be available in the future, and the "marketings" category is a short-term indicator of how much beef is ready to go to packers for slaughter. Today's feeder cattle become tomorrow's live cattle, so a glut or shortage in the number of cattle on feed or placed on feed affect live cattle prices down the road.

SUMMARY

How much the fundamentals affect the prices of commodity futures is a matter of debate. Most of the important fundamental numbers are calculated and predicted long before reports are released, and there are analysts whose sole purpose is to study the relevant product and make predictions. Many analysts release private reports for their clients. These predictions are also highly reported in the media, so there are usually no big surprises and the expectations of the report are priced into the market before it is released. Nevertheless, most traders do not like to hold big positions in a commodity that is awaiting a report in case there is a major upheaval.

The general wisdom is to use all of the tools at your disposal, so that if any of the fundamentals point in a certain direction, you can check the technical charts to see if that direction is confirmed or denied.

6

TECHNICAL ANALYSIS

"Those who cannot remember the past are condemned to repeat it."

– George Santayana

Technical analysis is the other method of trying to predict the commodity markets, using charts and graphs that track the movements of commodity prices. Technical analysts try to interpret patterns of past price movements and use them to project future movement based on those patterns. Technical analysis is used in other markets as well, since most people believe that history repeats itself. Some, but not all, technical traders ignore fundamental news and concentrate solely on the numbers. But most traders believe in finding a balance between the technical and fundamental elements of trading, combining accurate, fundamental knowledge with data from technical charts to create a clearer picture of what is happening in a market.

One of the major advantages of fundamental analysis is also its major disadvantage: the information is widely available and therefore widely discounted. The information that is not available to the average trader is probably only available to very large traders, so the average person only learns of it after the market has been impacted. One can imagine that Coca-Cola, Nestle, and Folger's have many ways of finding out what is going on every minute in, respectively, the sugar, cocoa, and coffee fields of the world. What the average person can know, however, is how each of the movements in the market affects future movements in the market. This is what technical trading tells us.

John Murphy, in his classic treatment of technical analysis, Technical Analysis of the Futures Markets, states that, "The technician believes that anything that can possibly affect the market price of a commodities futures contract — fundamental, political, psychological or otherwise — is actually reflected in the price of that commodity. It follows therefore that a study of price action is all that is required. By studying price charts and supporting technical indicators, the technician lets the market tell him which way it is most likely to go. The chartist knows there are reasons why markets go up and down. He just does not believe that knowing what those reasons are is necessary."

The field of technical analysis is a very deep and complex field, with thousands of theories about how technical moves should be interpreted and what additional tools can be employed to interpret those moves. Many books and treatises have been devoted to this topic, and it is truly a science unto itself. Devoting a chapter to it can only serve to explain the basic theories and how some of the tools are used. A trader interested in using technical analysis as a trading tool should devote additional in depth study to this intricate subject.

USING THE TECHNICAL CHARTS

The basic information on the technical charts and graphs are the opening price, highest price, lowest price, and closing price. These may be used on different graphs in different ways and in different combinations.

Using these charts, traders attempt to spot various patterns: long-term patterns, short-term patterns, patterns that occur over seasons, etc., and apply these patterns to their predictions of what should happen in the future. These patterns are used to determine the trend of a commodity's price, which is one of the most important concepts of technical trading. Of course, there is no guarantee that these patterns or trends will repeat themselves, but understanding the history of a given commodity is a good foundation for understanding how it should be traded. Traders also watch the relationship between the prices of the various delivery periods. "Backwardation," in the commodity futures world, means that nearby prices are higher than deferred prices. For some traders, this is a true signal of an important market shift because it indicates that supplies have become tight. Historical markets have shown that the classic manifestation of tight supplies, a steep backwardation, is when nearby prices (front months) are well above those for future delivery (back months). In other words, the principle of backwardation says that as the contract approaches expiration, the futures contract will trade at a higher price compared to when the contract was further away from expiration. This is said to occur due to the yield being higher than the current rate, which has little to no risk. When backwardation does occur in a market, it has been suggested that an individual in the short position would benefit the most by delivering as late as possible. Backwardation in futures was called "normal backwardation" by economist John Maynard Keynes. He believed that a price movement such as the one suggested by backwardation was not random but consistent with the market conditions.

Backwardation is the opposite of contango. Contango is a term used to describe the amount by which a commodity for future delivery is higher than nearer delivery. Contango is considered to be normal for non-perishable commodities that have a "cost of carry," such as warehousing fees and the opportunity costs of the money tied up. In theory, the contango should equal the cost of carry, because both producers and consumers can compare the futures contract price against the spot price plus storage, and choose the better one. But if there is a near-term shortage, this price comparison does not work, and the contango may be reduced or disappear altogether. When near prices become higher than far prices because for consumers future delivery does not suffice, of course, the market will shift back into backwardation. For perishable commodities or commodities that can expire, price differences between near and far delivery are not a contango. Different delivery dates are like different commodities in the case of perishable commodities, since fresh eggs today are not fresh in 6 months time, 90-day treasury bills will expire, etc.

The simplest chart or graph shows a trend, and thus attempts to form a pattern that indicates that the price of a commodity is moving steadily up or down. Trend lines are drawn between supports (a trend between the lowest prices) and resistance (a trend between highest prices).

Trends such as these can be short term (measured in days), or medium or long term (measured in weeks or month or even years).

The simplistic approach is as follows: If a new price falls below the support line (connecting the lows), the trend is down; if a new price falls above the resistance line (connecting the highs), the trend is up.

Other combined factors, such as the relationship between price and volume, or price and commercial activity, are monitored in technical analysis to predict price direction. An increase in the volume of commercial activity at the same time there is an increase in price may indicate a strong demand.

Technical analysts are concerned with what happened and not why. They look at movements of the past and the aftermath of those movements and try to find similar current movements, expecting similar aftermaths. Charts that go back months or years may show patterns that repeat themselves and the analysts take positions based on the continuation of that pattern. Technical trading is an extremely complex field with many, many different approaches, some using complicated mathematical formulas, but the purpose of each of them is the same: to predict the future based on the past.

THE CHARTS

The most common charts used in technical analysis are bar charts, candlestick charts, and point and figure charts. The most popular of all is a bar chart, which shows the action of the price as a thin vertical bar, with different information about the price indicated by small dashes along the length of the bar. With a chart such as this, a trader can spot at a glance the direction prices have taken and what the price activity during a chosen period was.

BAR CHART

The bottom of the chart is time movement and can represent minutes or years, with the daily, weekly, and monthly being the most popular charts. The timeframe can be changed readily to show prices over as long as two or 20-year timeframes (for historical perspectives), to hour or minute timeframes, which interest short-term traders. The range of prices is indicated on the right hand vertical scale. The bar represents the prices for the particular range of time: On a daily chart, the top of the bar would fall at the high for the day, and the bottom at the low. Extending slightly to the left and right of each bar are two small ticks; the tick to the left is the opening price and the tick to the right is the closing price. So on one line, we can see the high, low, open, and close for that day, if it is a daily chart. With a weekly bar chart, the top of the bar represents the high for the week, the bottom the low for the week, etc.

CANDLESTICK CHART

Understanding candlestick charts is a little more difficult, but the concept is the same. Candlestick charts are called that because that is what they look like — a shape with a wick sticking out of the top. The wider the price range of the commodity, the longer the candlestick will be. The top of the candle represents the opening, the bottom the close, the bar extending upward the high, the bar extending downward the low. The hollow or filled portion of the candlestick is called the "real body" and the thin lines above and below the body are the high/low range for the period and are called "shadows" (or wicks and tails). Hollow candlesticks mean that the close is greater than the open and indicate buying pressure. Filled candlesticks mean that the close is less than the open and indicate selling pressure. Many technical traders enjoy using candlestick charts because so much information can be seen at once.

POINT AND FIGURE CHARTS

Point and figure charts were widely used in the 1960s for the technical analysis of stocks, and were adapted to the analysis of commodities. At the turn of the 20th century, many investors in the stock market started to realize that certain stock patterns repeated themselves; as a result, point and figure analysis evolved as a simple, logical way to record share price movements. As can be seen in the sample point and figure chart below, columns marked by an X indicate periods when the stock was rising; columns including O show when the stock was falling.

SAMPLE POINT AND FIGURE CHART

Point and figure charts track daily price movements without factoring in the passage of time. X's indicate a rising price, O's indicate a falling price. In this way, non-significant price movements are filtered out, and the trader can more easily see support and resistance levels. Additional points are added if the price changes by more than a specific amount designated by the charter, which is represented by the size of the box. Each column consists of only one letter, either X or O, and new columns are only added if the price changes direction by more than the specified reversal amount. These kinds of charts are usually used in long-term trading, and proficient users of them believe they solidly indicate valid entry and exit points in a market.

HOW TO OBTAIN CHARTS

There are subscription chart services that allow traders to follow price movements; the price of the service is contingent upon the immediacy of the prices. There are computer programs that allow prices to be input, and the chart is created by the program. Or the trader can simply draw a price chart on a piece of graph paper. This may be the most efficient as well as the most cost-effective way for a new trader to get a feel for price movements. It certainly puts the trader in close contact with the movements of the market. The more dynamic and expensive solutions may or may not give an advantage to the trader. Remember that famous fortunes were made in commodities long before the advent of the computer. But it is important to realize that one of the basic tenets of commodity trading is the homogenization of information. All of the information in a market is available, processed and discounted by all participants. If other traders are working with more up-to-date information, a trader who is not works at a disadvantage, since one of the principles of commodity trading is the concept of readily available, shared information.

Whatever charting system is used, interpreting the patterns is the most important part of the system. Reading a chart is one thing; interpreting it is another. This is one of the reasons that volume and open interest numbers are added to the analysis, since they show the momentum and strength of the market.

HOW TO INTERPRET TECHNICAL CHARTS

There are three main types of chart patterns: double bottoms and double tops, big W's (or the opposite, big M's) and flags. A double bottom or a double top will confirm a movement if it moves within certain percentages. The wider or narrower the valleys created by these bottoms also give important information about the direction of the market, and traders especially watch the volume traded as occurs at the point of bottoms or tops. An uptrend will lead to a double top, and acts as a confirmation. A Big W or Big M pattern includes double bottoms with extremely tall sides, and breaking through patterns such as this will indicate

Double Bottom	Big W	Flag
Double Top	Big M	High, Tight Flag

extremely strong support for that direction. Flags can indicate three directions: down slope, up slope, and horizontal. Flags show a compact channel of price movement and therefore direction. It can get much more complicated than this — for example, following the two parts of the flag, the flagpole, and the flag itself. The flagpole shows a steep uptrend and the flag indicates the consolidation period of prices, in the tight channel area. The Head and Shoulders

Pattern indicates price movements by testing the resistance level of prices. As can be seen in the example, the price first rises to a peak and then subsequently declines, rises above the former peak and again declines and then finally rises again, but not to the second peak, and then declines again. The first and third peaks are shoulders, and the second peak is the head.

All charts are used to measure trends, but the timeframe of the trend that is being measured can vary greatly. Time frames of minutes, hours, days, weeks, months, and years are all used consistently and are compared to each other to confirm movements and trends. The basic measurement on the chart is the price, but some analysts like to view the price movements as they compare with other statistics such as volume or open interest.

A day trader will watch very short-term movements to look for entry and exit points in inter day trading to make a quick profit. Longer term traders look at the commodity charts that cover weeks, months, or even years. Beginners should start with the long-term charts to get a feel for how a given commodity has traded over time. Historical charts such as this can be obtained at **finance.yahoo.com**.

SUPPORT AND RESISTANCE

There are charting services that do the analysis of the charts, but for a basic beginner lesson, it may be interesting to simply look at the chart to spot patterns. Charts are intended to show the continual interaction between the buyers and sellers in the market. This interaction creates certain price levels known as support and resistance. When buyers continue to bid up the price of a commodity, the price level will continue to stay at or above a certain price. When it does this for any length of time (the length of time depends on the timeframe of the chart), it is considered to be a support price, indicating that the price will not fall below this support, but should continue rising. Resistance is the opposite: When buyers offer less and less for a commodity, the price will fall back down each time it hits this resistance line, and appear unable to break through it. Technical traders find these support and resistance levels by drawing a line across a series of prices (again, depending on the timeframe of the chart). Eventually, what these support and resistance lines form is a "trend line." This is the crux of technical trading. If a trader can identify a trend and follow it until it ends, or reverses, he will make a profit. If he identifies an uptrend, he will buy and hold the commodity until the charts indicate some resistance, which will be a signal to him that the trend is weakening and it is time for him to liquidate the position at a profit. If he has identified a downtrend, he will be a seller of a commodity and hold his short position until price support has been identified and he can buy the contracts back at a much lower price before the prices start to increase once again.

VOLUME

Another important indicator in charting commodities prices is volume. Trading volume is the amount of trading activity in a given commodity. If volume increases just at the point of a significant increase in the price of the commodity, this will indicate an increased interest by investors in buying and holding the commodity, and that prices should continue to rise. If volume is increasing while the prices are falling, you would not want to be long in the commodity, since this would indicate that investors are getting rid of the commodity, and the price will continue to fall. Volume is considered an important confirming indicator in commodities trading. Volume normally precedes price. It is important to make sure that the heavier volume is taking place in the direction of the trend. A firm uptrend will be indicated by rising volume combined with rising open interest.

TRENDLINES

The trendline is the most important of the charting tools. The trendline is designed to indicate a trend in a given market. If a trader follows a trendline until it ends, he should make money. These are the indications that traders glean from the trends in the charts:

- **Uptrend:** The market is moving higher. In an uptrend, the market will tend to make higher lows and higher highs.

- **Downtrend:** The market is moving lower. In a downtrend, the market will tend to make lower highs and lower lows.

It is easy to see how markets move in trends. Moves of any significance are seen in series of higher highs/higher lows or lower highs/lower lows. The trend line is drawn on the chart following the tops or bottoms of the price bars that lead in the direction of the trend. In a rising market, the trendline would be seen connecting the higher lows.

To validate the trend, at least two major points should be determined. In a falling market, the line would connect two or more highs. The more points that are connected, the more valid the trend is considered. As a rule of thumb, a really strong trendline should touch at least three previous highs or lows. The more points the line catches, the better the line. The problem with this analysis is that the more points you have, the more data you have to have and therefore the trendline may already be old and ready to end. A broken trendline (a price action moving below an up trendline or above a down trendline) signals that a tread has reversed. If an up trendline is broken, long positions should be liquidated and short positions established. If a down trendline is broken, short positions should be liquidated and long positions established. If the market quickly resumes its old direction after a trendline break, a new trendline should be drawn using the new significant high or low points.

CHANNELS

Channels are identified by drawing a line parallel to a major trendline. If a market is trending higher, and an uptrendline has been identified, the top line of the channel is drawn by connecting the progressive highs. (In a downtrend, the parallel line would connect the progressive lows.) This creates the channel and as long as prices remain within the channel, the market is continuing its trend. If a market trades outside of the channel, this should be viewed as a signal to some change in the market. In general, when market trades above the upper channel line in an uptrend or below the lower channel line in a downtrend, the market is probably starting an accelerated phase. Strong breakouts of channels will usually see the market move quickly, with accelerated price movements.

BREAKOUTS

Breakouts are one of the strongest indicators that technical traders use. A breakout is the dramatic movement of the price of a commodity out of its normal trading area. It will normally be a significant percentage move, accompanied by a massive increase in trading volume. Usually, breakouts occur as a result of unexpected events or surprises in the market. It is very rare that a breakout on strong volume with a large percentage move fizzles out and moves back to normal trading areas, even though some breakouts do not continue up or down immediately, and false breakouts do occur, but they are probably more a result of misinterpretation of the signals. Breakouts are based on support and resistance levels.

Support: Demand is strong enough to prevent the price from going lower. Support levels can be seen where buying interest has been seen before, and should be expected to be seen again. If the market does not hold onto this direction, it is said to be breaking support, and the market can be expected to trade lower.

Resistance: Selling is strong enough to prevent the price from rising any further. This is the level at which the market has a hard time moving higher. If a price hits the resistance level and then falls back, it is said to be hitting the resistance level.

Support and resistance levels are drawn horizontally through the ceiling (in the case of resistance) or floor (in the case of support) points.

In a breakout, a price passes through, and stays through, either a support or resistance level. The support and resistance levels represent important data in technical trading. If a market trades in a flat range, where it consistently holds at the support levels and fails at the resistance level, it is said to be in consolidation. When a market fails at resistance a number of times and then trades above it, it indicates that buying interest has finally outpaced selling interest and the price will break out of consolidation. The opposite happens if a support level is broken. Of course, false breakouts can occur which can be very frustrating to a trader; he would have liquidated the position he was holding for the trend, only to see the same trend resume, this time without his position in place.

GUIDELINES FOR TRADING BREAKOUTS

Following a false breakout is happens to all traders at some point, but following certain guidelines help you avoid it too often.

- The longer it takes to form a consolidation, the more significant the breakout and the larger the move will be that follows it. In other words, a breakout on a weekly chart has more significance than a breakout on a daily chart. A breakout on an annual chart signifies a major balance disruption in that market.

- After a breakout, the price should not trade back into the consolidation zone. If it does, it is probably a false breakout.

- The breakout should remain above the breakout level for a period of time. If it falls back down quickly, it is probably a false breakout.

- A true breakout is usually associated with a sharp rise in volume. False breakouts usually have modest volumes.

- If stops are used, they should not be placed just under support or just above resistance. It is better to take a little more risk and give the stops some room before they will be exercised.

- Use the count. Technical traders follow a rule that says when a market breaks out from a consolidation, it will move about the same distance up or down equal to the horizontal distance of the consolidation phase. In other words, measure the length of the consolidation phase and then draw that same distance up, to find the upward price of the breakout, or down to find the downward price of the breakout.

HEAD AND SHOULDERS

Head and shoulders patterns are classic reverse patterns that signal that a major top or bottom is forming. Once a trader identifies a head and shoulder pattern, it is time to take profits, cut losses, or establish a new position based on the indicated direction. The head and shoulders pattern is most often seen in an uptrend and is considered most reliable when found in an uptrend. The head is a price peak, with another peak lower than the head to the left (left shoulder) and another peak lower than the head to the right (right shoulder).

Head and Shoulders Top

A head and shoulders is indicated when the left shoulder and the head are in place, and the market starts to rally from the neck. The right shoulder forms when the market fails at a lower high than the major high. The classic pattern for a head and shoulders is when the right shoulder is of approximately the same size and extent as the left shoulder, but this is not always the case. A head and shoulders pattern is not complete until the right shoulder has completely formed and the decline from the right shoulder's peak breaks under the neckline. Sellers should enter the market at the highs (left shoulder) and the downside has been probed (beginning neckline). Buyers should enter the market and ultimately push through to new highs to form the head. However, the new highs are quickly turned back and the downside is tested again, which continues the neckline. Tentative buying will then occur to cause another rally, but one that fails to take out the previous high. (This last top is considered the right shoulder.) Buying dries up and the market tests the downside yet again. The trendline for this pattern should be drawn from the beginning neckline to the continuing neckline. Even though volume is important in all-trend patterns, volume has more importance in the head and shoulders patterns versus other patterns. Volume generally follows the price higher on the left shoulder. The head, however, is formed on diminished volume; this indicates that buyers are not as aggressive as they once were. On the last rallying attempt — the left shoulder — volume is even lighter than on the head, signaling that the buyers may have exhausted themselves. New sellers enter and previous buyers exit. This pattern is complete when the market breaks the neckline. Volume usually increases on the breakout.

The head and shoulders pattern can sometimes be inverted. The inverted head and shoulders is normally seen in downtrends. One of the major differences in the inverted head and shoulders is the volume. The inverted left shoulder is still accompanied by an increase in volume and the inverted head shows lighter volume. The rally from the head, however, should show greater volume than the rally from the left shoulder. Finally, the inverted right shoulder should register the lightest volume of all. When the market then rallies through the neckline, a big increase in volume should be seen.

Guidelines for Trading Head and Shoulders

- Do not try to anticipate a head and shoulders pattern. You may see what is really not there if you force the issue. Wait until the pattern is complete before it is traded.

- The longer a head and shoulders pattern takes to develop, and the more pronounced the pattern, the stronger the resulting move will be.

- Once the market breaks the neckline, watch for a return move back to the neckline.

- The slope of the neckline has important information. Downward sloping necklines for head and shoulders tops mean greater odds for a bear move to follow; upward sloping necklines for inverted head and shoulders bottoms mean greater odds for a bull market to follow.

- Pay close attention to volume.

- If the head forms a complete "island" (the above illustration is a good example), the validity of the signal is strongly increased.

- A complete pattern should act in a predictable way. If it starts to act incorrectly, it is time to recognize a false signal and exit the market.

TOPS AND BOTTOMS

Double tops and bottoms may form when the market tests either the market highs or market lows. These patterns are frequently associated with major tops and bottoms. In a double top, prices peak, retrace downward, and peak again at roughly the same price level. This pattern is a strong indicator of a downturn in the price trend. It is an even stronger indicator if the double top touches an established resistance level. A double bottom is the reverse of a double top.

Rounded tops and bottoms are one of the most reliable reversal patterns. Rounded bottoms are elongated and U-shaped, and are sometimes referred to as bowls or saucers. A Rounded Bottom is considered a bullish signal, indicating a possible reversal of the current downtrend to a new uptrend. The pattern is confirmed when the price breaks out above its moving average. A rounded top forms the shape of an upside down "U." A rounding top may form at the end of an extended upward trend and indicates a reversal in the long-term price movement. The pattern can develop over several weeks, months, or even years. Rounded tops and bottoms do not occur very often.

FLAGS, PENNANTS, AND GAPS

Flags: Indicate a straight up or down move that is either completely vertical or at least very steep. A flag is a short consolidation that has parallel boundaries that point either upward or downward. A flagpole is first formed because of large volume on a major trend. The flag represents a pause in the trend before it continues. The flag should, in general, run in the opposite direction of the general trend. In other words, a flag will be blowing upwards for a downtrend and downwards for an uptrend. But this is not always the case and it is important to watch the movement immediately after the formation of a flag.

Pennants: Indicate converging trendlines that occur during market consolidation. Prior to a breakout, a pennant will occur at weakening volume followed by a large increase in volume. In a pennant, the boundaries are not parallel.

Gaps: A gap is indicated when a commodity opens at a price higher than the high of the previous day or lower than the low of the previous day. A gap is considered intact as long as the gap is not filled during the trading session — the market never trades low enough to equal the high of the previous day or high enough to equal the low of the previous day. Most gaps are filled during the trading day, or within a day or two. It is important to determine what kind of gap is occurring. They normally fall into one of three categories:

- A breakaway gap will appear as a market is breaking out into a new trend. Breakaway gaps appear suddenly on a chart, and signal a new move. An upside breakaway gap will occur when prices jump up from a bottom; a downside breakaway gap occurs when prices jump down from a top. Both of these usually occur after some kind of consolidation, as seen above. A breakaway gap indicates pressure to push a market to the next level that is so strong it has to literally jump to that level. In this way, many market participants are stuck on the wrong side. Traders trapped on the wrong side add fuel to this trend because they have to liquidate. Shorts trapped by an upside breakaway gap have positions at a loss and need to cover, and longs trapped above a downside breakaway will have to sell, confirming the downside trend. Breakaway gaps are not filled for a long time, unlike an ordinary gap that will fill quickly. A trader should recognize and trade the new trend on a breakaway gap.

- Continuation gaps show about halfway through trends, when enthusiasm for climbing prices or fear of receding prices overpowers reason. They appear just where traders think the price should reverse. Most markets fill many continuation gaps for at least a bar or two before they reverse. Traders should place their orders within this extreme price level. The order may not get filled, but the trader will avoid entering too early.

- An exhaustion gap forms near the end of a move. Exhaustion gaps burn out trends with one last surge of energy. In an uptrend, the market will gap to a new high, usually on major bullish news. In a downtrend the market gaps to a new low, either on bearish news, or panic selling. Exhaustion gaps need to be watched closely as an indicator of the next move.

Guidelines for Trading Gaps

- Most gaps are common gaps. Assume a gap will be filled; if it is not filled within a few days, it can be treated as a significant gap.

- Breakaway gaps appear suddenly. Placing a sell stop at the low end of the gap will cover you if necessary, but if it is a strong breakaway gap, it will not be filled.

- Do not anticipate exhaustion gaps. Since they occur at the final stage of a major move, it is best to wait out the market and determine a new move.

- Once a gap has been firmly identified, move quickly.

OTHER INDICATORS

In addition to watching the patterns that form as prices move, technical traders keep an eye on what is happening in the markets as these patterns are forming. Volume, open interest, and relative strength index (RSI), moving averages, oscillators, Bollinger Bands, and wave theory all help to support or negate the patterns and trends found in the movements on the charts.

VOLUME

Volume is simply the number of contracts traded during a specified time frame (e.g., hour, day, week, month) of the chart being analyzed. The analysis of volume is a basic yet very important element of technical analysis. Volume provides clues as to the intensity of a given price move. Volume is a very significant signal to technical traders. Significant moves are usually associated with significant volume. In general, low volume levels signify indecision in the market that typically occurs during consolidation periods (i.e., periods when prices move sideways in a trading range). Low volume also often occurs during the indecisive period during market bottoms.

High volume levels indicate market tops when there is a strong consensus that prices will move higher. High volume levels are also very common at the beginning of new trends (for example, breakouts). Just before market bottoms, volume will often increase due to panic-driven selling. Volume can help determine the health of an existing trend. As a general rule of thumb, a strong uptrend should have higher volume on the upward legs of the trend, and lower volume on the downward legs. A strong downtrend usually has higher volume on the downward legs of the trend and lower volume on the upward legs.

Volume is an essential part of every technical formation, since each pattern usually has a volume pattern attached to it. If the volume pattern does not align with price, then the interpretation of the price pattern is not trustworthy. For example, as discussed above, the volume pattern for a head and shoulders top formation is very distinctive. On the left shoulder, volume reaches a peak. As prices move up to the head, volume increases, but this second volume peak should be lower than that of the left shoulder. If the volume chart is different than the one just described, then the price pattern may appear to be a head and shoulders, but is in fact not.

Guidelines for Using Volume

- Volume will tend to be higher on rallies and lower on declines when a market is in an uptrend.

- Volume will tend to be higher on declines and lower on rallies when a market is in a downtrend.

- Volume increases dramatically at major tops and bottoms.

OPEN INTEREST

The total number of open contracts on a commodity is called open interest. Each contract has a buyer, who holds a long position, and a seller, who holds a short position. The open interest number is the total number of longs and the total number of shorts. It is often used to confirm trends and trend reversals for futures and options contracts. The open-interest position that is reported each day represents the increase or decrease in the number of contracts for that day, and it is shown as a positive or negative number. An increase in open interest along with an increase in price is said to confirm an upward trend. Similarly, an increase in open interest along with a decrease in price confirms a downward trend. An increase or decrease in prices while open interest remains flat or declining may indicate a possible trend reversal. Here is the concept in action: A market is moving lower, yet open interest is increasing. Obviously, some traders will leave the market at this lower price, but they are being replaced by new buyers. If new buyers were not entering the market, the open interest would drop. Like just about all concepts in technical trading, open interest follows certain rules based on historical observations. Famed chartist Martin Pring in his book Martin Pring on Market Momentum sums them up perfectly:

1. If prices are rising and open interest is increasing at a rate faster than its five-year seasonal average, this is a bullish sign. More participants are entering the market, involving additional buying, and any purchases are generally aggressive in nature.

2. If the open-interest numbers flatten following a rising trend in both price and open interest, take this as a warning sign of an impending top.

3. High open interest at market tops is a bearish signal if the price drop is sudden, since this will force many "weak" longs to liquidate. Occasionally, such conditions set off a self-feeding, downward spiral.

4. An unusually high or record open interest in a bull market is a danger signal. When a rising trend of open interest begins to reverse, expect a bear trend to get underway.

5. A breakout from a trading range will be much stronger if open interest rises during the consolidation. This is because many traders will be caught on the wrong side of the market when the breakout finally takes place. When the price moves out of the trading range, these traders are forced to abandon their positions. It is possible to take this rule one step further and say the greater the rise in open interest during the consolidation, the greater the potential for the subsequent move.

6. Rising prices and a decline in open interest at a rate greater than the seasonal norm is bearish. This market condition develops because short covering and not fundamental demand is fueling the rising price trend. In these circumstances money is flowing out of the market. Consequently, when the short covering has run its course, prices will decline.

7. If prices are declining and the open interest rises more than the seasonal average, this indicates that new short positions are being opened. As long as this process continues it is a bearish factor, but once the shorts begin to cover it turns bullish.

8. A decline in both price and open interest indicates liquidation by discouraged traders with long positions. As long as this trend continues, it is a

bearish sign. Once open interest stabilizes at a low level, the liquidation is over and prices are then in a position to rally again.

RELATIVE STRENGTH INDEX (RSI)

Oscillators are a group of indicators that technical traders use to indicate overbought or oversold conditions. The most commonly used oscillator is the relative strength index (RSI), which measures the velocity of a price. The RSI measures the rate of change of the commodity's price by comparing the average price change of its increases with the average price change of its decreases. RSI is also called the momentum oscillator because it indicates the momentum or speed that a price is rising or falling. It is calculated using the average gain of the days the commodity closes higher divided by the average gain of the days the commodity closes lower. Technical traders look to the RSI to tell them whether a given commodity is overbought or oversold. The actual formula is RSI = 100 - (100/1 = RS), where RS is the average of net up closing changes (for whatever number of days are being measured) divided by the average of net down closing changes. For example, to calculate the RSI over the past week, you would average the change of the previous seven days and divide this number by the average of the change of the seven days before that. The RSI usually fluctuates between 25 and 75 when there is pressure, it may move under 25 or over 75; under 25 would mean that a commodity is becoming oversold, and demand will push the price up and over 75 would mean that it is becoming overbought, and supply will push the price down. One of the dangers of using the RSI as an indicator is that in very volatile markets, it can remain oversold or overbought for long periods of time. Because of this, it is difficult to trade using RSI numbers alone, but the RSI is a very good indictor of upcoming reversal points. Once the RSI price starts moving in one direction or the other, be prepared to buy if the RSI starts heading into an oversold range, or sell if it indicates that the market is overbought, as long as the other indictors you are using support this.

MOVING AVERAGES

Technical traders also examine moving averages. This is the average of the price of a commodity over a period of time. They may look at both the simple moving average and the enhanced moving average. The simple moving average calculates the closing price of a commodity over a period of time, divided by the period of time. To calculate the 30-day simple moving average of corn, one would add all of the closing prices for those 30 days and then divide the total by 30. The enhanced moving average is said to be more accurate since it gives a higher weight to the most recent prices and therefore older activity in the commodity is discounted to some extent. Moving averages are used to confirm if a trend is still in motion, or it has changed. They are not good advance indicators of a change in a trend movement, but serve best to confirm a direction or change in direction. Many technical traders use combination charts that use two moving averages to confirm a signal. When the shorter average line crosses the longer average line (a four and nine day average, for example, or a nine and eighteen day average), a confirmation of the trend is signaled.

Moving averages are one of the most popular tools used in interpreting charts. As a matter of fact, George Kleinman, in Trading Commodities and Financial Futures, calls it the most valuable technical tool ever. There are many types of moving averages, but the concept is the same in all of them: They track trends by smoothing out the day-to-day price fluctuations.

The simplest form of a moving average is the simple moving average (SMA). It is calculated by taking the arithmetic mean of a set of values (prices). For example, to calculate a 10-day simple moving average, you would add up the closing prices from the past 10 days and then divide the result by 10. The resulting average takes into account the past 10 data points in order to give traders an idea of how a commodity is priced relative to the past 10 days. It is called a moving average because, as new values become available, the oldest data points are dropped from the equation and new data points are added to replace them. This ensures that only the most recent information is included. Once the values of the moving average have been calculated, they are plotted onto a price chart and then connected to create a moving average line. These curving lines are very common on the technical trading charts, but there are different ways to use them. It is possible to add more than one moving average to a chart by adjusting the number of time periods used in the calculations.

The simple moving average is popular among traders, but it has its limitations, since each point in the data series has exactly the same weight in the overall calculation, no matter where it occurs in the sequence. Many analysts believe that the more recent the data, the more significant it is, and therefore should have a greater influence on the final calculation than older data. This led to the development of different types of moving averages that give more weight to more recent data. The most popular of these types of moving averages is the exponential moving average (EMA). The exponential moving average gives more weight to recent prices so that it is more responsive to new information. Understanding the equation for calculating an EMA is probably unnecessary, since nearly all charting packages do the calculations for you.

Moving averages are a totally customizable indicator, since the trader can freely choose the timeframe in creating the average. The most common time periods used in moving averages are 15, 20, 30, 50, 100, and 200 days. Obviously, the shorter the time span used to create the average, the more sensitive it will be to price changes and, conversely, the longer the time span, the less sensitive, or more "smooth," the average will be. There is no right or wrong timeframe to use when setting up moving averages; it will depend upon the trading strategy.

The main function of moving averages is to identify trends and reversals, measure the strength of the price momentum, and help determine the most likely areas where a commodity price will find support or resistance. In this way they can be a very important part of an overall trading strategy. Moving averages are lagging indicators, which means that they do not predict new trends, but confirm trends once they have been established. A commodity is thought to be in an uptrend when the price is above a moving average and the average is sloping upward. On the other hand, a trader will use a price below a downward sloping average to confirm a downtrend. Many traders only consider holding a long position in a commodity when the price is trading above a moving average. This rule helps them ensure that the trend is working in their favor. Remember, most traders do not try to catch a price at the top or the bottom, but follow the trend on its way up or down before a reversal.

One of the best methods to determine the strength and direction of a commodity price momentum is to use three moving averages superimposed upon a chart and then pay close attention to how they stack up in relation to one another. The three moving averages generally have varying timeframes to represent short-term, medium-term and long-term price movements. Strong upward momentum is seen when shorter-term averages are located above longer-term averages and the two averages are diverging. Conversely, when the shorter-term averages are located below the longer-term averages, the momentum is in the downward direction.

STOCHASTIC OSCILLATOR

The stochastic oscillator is a momentum indicator that shows the location of the current close relative to the high/low range over a set number of periods. Closing levels that are consistently near the top of the range indicate accumulation (buying pressure) and those near the bottom of the range indicate distribution (selling pressure). The stochastic oscillator is not a normalized relative strength indicator, like most other momentum oscillators. It compares the price of a tradable commodity to its price range over a period of time. It tells you where the current closing price is relative to the recent range of the commodity. There are three types of Stochastic Oscillators: Fast, Slow, and Full. These oscillators are calculated using a formula, and the resulting measurement is placed on a chart to indicate what the oscillator is doing at the time of given price movements. (Most traders do not calculate these formulas themselves, but only understand them so they can interpret a stochastic oscillator indicated on a chart. Most charting services will indicate these oscillators.) Readings below 20 are considered oversold and readings above 80 are considered overbought. A reading below 20 or a reading above 80 is not automatically bearish or bullish, but rather can be used as a signal when the oscillator moves from overbought territory back below 80 and from oversold territory back above 20, in other words, when divergence occurs.

The most important thing to note about the stochastic oscillator as an indicator is the original intention behind it. Originally, George Lane, its creator, stated that divergence was the only valid signal on which to trade. One of the most reliable signals is to wait for a divergence to develop from overbought or oversold levels. Once the oscillator reaches overbought levels, wait for a negative divergence to develop and then cross below 80. This usually requires a double dip below 80 and the second dip results in the sell signal. For a buy signal, wait for a positive divergence to develop after the indicator moves below 20. This will usually require a trader to disregard the first break above 20. After a positive divergence forms, the second break above 20 confirms the divergence and a buy signal is given.

BOLLINGER BANDS

A last tool to discuss is Bollinger Bands, developed by analyst John Bollinger in the early 1980s. They arose from the need for adaptive trading bands and the observation that volatility was dynamic, not static as was widely believed at the time. Bollinger Bands are fluctuating bands that follow the price movement of a commodity. Bollinger Bands consist of a set of three curves drawn in relation to prices. The primary or middle band is a simple moving average. The middle band is a measure of the intermediate-term trend that serves as the base for the upper and lower bands. The interval between the upper and lower bands and the middle band is determined by volatility, typically the standard deviation of the same data that were used for the average. The default parameters, 20 periods and two standard deviations, may be adjusted to suit the trader's purposes. The second band is the upper band and is plotted by using the simple moving average plus two standard deviation units. (Standard deviation units are used in statistics as measures of volatility.) The third or lower band is the simple moving average minus two standard deviations. Here is what the Bollinger Bands are comprised of:

Middle Bollinger Band	= 20-period simple moving average
Upper Bollinger Band	= Middle Bollinger Band +2*20-period standard deviation
Lower Bollinger Band	= Middle Bollinger Band -2*20-period standard deviation

The idea behind Bollinger Bands is that they move in tandem with the moving average and track the price of the commodity on a relative basis. When a commodity price is volatile, the Bollinger Bands will expand; when prices are stable, Bollinger Bands contract. When the price of the commodity approaches the upper Bollinger Band, it indicates an overbought condition and the price of the commodity theoretically should come down; when the price approaches the lower Bollinger Band, there is an oversold condition and the price should increase. The purpose of Bollinger Bands is to provide a relative definition of high and low. By definition, prices are high at the upper band and low at the lower band. This definition can aid in pattern recognition and is useful in comparing price action to the action of indicators to arrive at systematic trading decisions. Two important tools are derived from the Bollinger Bands: BandWidth, a relative measure of the width of the bands, and %b, a measure of where the last price is in relation to the bands. The indicator %b tells us where we are within the bands. Unlike stochastics, which are bounded by 0 and 100, %b can assume negative values and values above 100 when prices are outside of the bands. At 100 we are at the upper band, at 0 we are at the lower band. Above 100 we are above the upper bands and below 0 we are below the lower band.

BandWidth = (Upper Bollinger Band)/Middle Bollinger Band
%b = (Last Bollinger Band)/(Upper Bollinger Band - Lower Bollinger Band)

BandWidth is most often used to quantify The Squeeze, a volatility-based trading opportunity. %b is used to clarify trading patterns and as an input for trading systems

("Bollinger on Bollinger Bands" by John Bollinger.) The use of Bollinger Bands varies among traders. Some traders buy when a price touches the lower Bollinger Band and sell when a price touches the moving average in the center of the bands. Other traders buy when a price breaks above the upper Bollinger Band or sell when a price falls below the lower Bollinger Band. Options traders often sell options when Bollinger Bands are historically far apart or buy options when the Bollinger Bands are historically close together, in both instances, expecting volatility to revert back toward the average historical volatility level for the commodity.

Here is a recap of some general trading rules using technical analysis:

1. Most markets have predictable trends and repeated patterns. Most commodity trading movements in the markets are a result of the motivations of people in those markets.

2. Look for important resistance and support validations on weekly charts and note the trend, then see if you have any of the same patterns on the daily charts.

3. Once a pattern has been established, look for breaks of support or resistance. Trying to predict these movements is useless; you have to wait for the move to get underway and get a confirmation via a stochastic indicator that will show that the odds of the trend continuing are high.

4. Manage your stops. Do not move stops too soon; put your stops below breakout point and move immediately if the position moves your way.

5. Most major trends develop from market highs.

6. In bull markets sell signals will not always work, and in bear markets buy signals will not always work. This is why a trader should always be ready to re-examine and exit positions that are not proving themselves, despite the technical data.

ELLIOT WAVE THEORY

Wave theory employs the age-old concept of history repeating itself. (Actually, most technical analyses use this theory, but none so explicitly as wave theory.) Besides trying to measure exactly what will happen in a given commodity market, we need to find when it will happen. In real estate, they say that location is everything; in commodity trading, they say that timing is everything. We have to remember that we are working in a highly leveraged market. The tiniest blip, made at the right or wrong time, will mean many multiples of dollars earned or lost. Perfect timing of entry and exit points in a market will translate into thousands of dollars gained or lost. The Elliot Wave Theory states that prices recur in market cycles comprised of impulse waves and corrective waves. If you picture the waves in the ocean, one observes that they usually come in patterns of three. According to the Elliot Wave Theory, impulse waves come in patterns of five, while corrective waves come in patterns of three. If you look at any chart, you can see a pattern that emulates waves. Even if a pattern is tracing steadily upward, one can observe "wave," or up and down patterns during this supposedly steady upward trend. The rules for figuring out the count for the Elliot Wave Theory are as follows:

1. Wave 2 should not break below the beginning of Wave 1.

2. Wave 3 should not be the shortest wave among Waves 1, 3, and 5.

3. Wave 4 should not overlap with Wave 1, except for Waves 1, 5, a, or c or a higher degree.

4. Rule of alternation: Waves 2 and 4 should unfold in two different waveforms.

Obviously, this is a bit complicated to use, but understanding it is important. Many traders use wave theory for market timing decisions. Even if you don't use the wave theory and count the waves yourself, be aware of technical analyses that advise when a wave theory is poised to tell you when to enter or exit a market. Even if you decide not to use this timing system, you will have invaluable information, knowing that other traders, including the big ones, are using these points as their buy and sell signals.

FUNDAMENTAL VS. TECHNICAL ANALYSIS

Which is best, fundamental or technical analysis? Most traders use both. They may rely more on fundamentals, and then look at the charts to see if they confirm what future trend the fundamentals are indicating, or they may watch their charts and then look at news to see what fundamental condition was occurring when a given price movement occurred. Some markets are more predictable and lend themselves better to charting, and some are so volatile that quick and erratic price movements become almost impossible to chart. Even purely fundamental analysts still examine chart movements. If market participants are using charts to manage their positions and their trades, their actions will influence the market. Anything that influences the market is a fundamental, and in this way charting almost becomes a fundamental.

In other words, integrating both fundamental and technical analysis into a trading philosophy is probably the most prudent way to trade. What is more difficult, and probably more important, is how to separate the wheat from the chaff. There is so much information out there, and the more one starts to research, the more information one will find. We mentioned that, for the most part, commodities are the abandoned asset class; most people are not familiar enough with commodities to include them in their portfolios. However, for those who have decided to include them, there is such an abundance of information available that one has to choose wisely between which information one should trust, which information one should use sparingly or discriminately, and which information one should discard entirely.

Taking a break from all of the details may be the order of the day at this point. If you have decided to primarily trade on technical, have a look at the fundamentals to confirm, or at least give you perspective. If you work with the fundamentals most of the time, take a step back and see what the technical indicators are saying.

What kinds of information do the consistently successful traders use? Governmental reports are always important to fundamental traders, and some technical traders rely on one technical system more than another. But markets change constantly and so does the information relevant to them, so most wise traders do not operate in a vacuum, but rather anticipate which information is going to have the most value for them in a particular market and at a particular time. Probably more important than any factor is not so much understanding the factors but instead how the market (read: other investors) will interpret those factors. The key is not only understanding all of the technical and fundamental factors, but also understanding and anticipating the psychology of the players and how the rest of the market will react to those factors. If you are accustomed to trading in the stock market, then you know that the stock market is expected to go up if the unemployment rate goes down, but then the market drops even with good "job numbers" because the numbers were anticipated and the market looked for other factors to react to. This happens more frequently, and with more intensity, in the commodity markets each and every day, since there are so many factors that influence them. The traders who understand the more significant factors in any given market and learn how to interpret them will have more consistent success.

PITFALLS

7

"Two things are infinite: the universe and human stupidity;
and I'm not sure about the universe."

— *Albert Einstein*

Commodity markets are not for everyone. It takes discipline
and stamina to follow a trading strategy while recognizing
when it is time to liquidate a position. Surveys have shown
that 90% of people stop trading within about a year,
due to lack of success. The ones who are successful and
remain in the market have found that overcoming certain
pitfalls and sticking to a trading plan yields profits over
an extended period of trades. Those who think they can
find a trading "secret" to predict prices and outsmart
other market participants are deluding themselves, and
probably spending a fortune on these so-called secret
systems. Promoters of such systems will always be able
to cite examples of how successful the system was by
using certain fixed examples. Testing the system over an
extended period of time is the only way to be sure that a
trading system works. For the most part in using these
secret systems, the only ones getting rich are the ones who
sell these trading systems.

Many people believe that if they have traded stocks successfully, they should be able to move into the more lucrative commodity market. But there are big differences between the stock market and the commodity market.

Unlike the stock market, where all of the investors in a company gain or lose together, in commodities, for every dollar gained by one trader, a dollar is lost by another. One trading rule is that funds traded on commodity markets should be "discretionary" income, that is, funds that you can afford to lose. Commodities are highly leveraged and a trader can lose more than his entire investment, especially if he gets locked into it by "limit moves." These happen occasionally in a number of commodities. The more typical problem for traders, however, is cumulative loss. Therefore, having recognized the intrinsic risks involved in trading commodities, there are other behavioral risks an aspiring trader should understand and avoid.

The seven deadly sins recognized by philosophers and religious leaders may be pride, envy, greed, laziness, gluttony, wrath, and lust, but the four critical ones for traders that can ruin a career in commodity trading are pride, envy, greed, and laziness. In trading, they translate into not cutting losses (too proud to admit a mistake), ignoring good judgment in using tools and strategies (envy that others are making a killing), not taking profits when you should (greed), and not keeping on top of the market at all times (laziness). We won't concern ourselves with the other vices the trader may exhibit in his off hours.

PRIDE

Too many traders let their losses run rather than getting out of a losing position and taking time to step back and re-evaluate the market. They have so thoroughly convinced themselves that the position they took was correct, and that the market will turn in their direction at any moment, that they continue to rack up losses. Many traders fall into the trap of "talking their book": They view the markets in terms of their positions instead of the other way around, and are able to cogently argue the validity of their continued position. Fundamental factors can be interpreted in many ways, so a trader may interpret them to support the argument that his position is still correct. But this has even been known to happen when a trader uses technical analysis, using a time frame to explain things away, or spotting a trend or a pattern that is not really there in order to support his view.

ENVY

Many people hear those apocryphal stories of vast profits being made in commodities in a short time. There are many such cases, such as George Soros, who made $2 billion in one week in 1992 (and $2 billion in 1992 was a LOT of money) by borrowing $10 billion to bet against the British pound. But even rich and knowledgeable can be wiped out. In another famous commodity trading legend, the billionaire Hunt family saw their fortune disappear practically overnight when they tried to take over the silver market in the late 1970s. The price of silver rose on their buying, following the price law of demand, but it crashed, dropping to $10 per ounce from a peak of $50. The Hunts lost $1.3 billion. Trying to do what everyone else is doing because they seem to be doing better will bring a trader down fast. The only antidote is discipline, such as using techniques such stop-loss orders or limit orders. This will bring more consistent success than trying to emulate the big guys, who may be on their way down.

GREED

Gordon Gekko, in the movie Wall Street, avowed that "Greed is good." Whether or not it was ever true on Wall Street, it is definitely not true in the world of commodities. When it gets out of control, greed is one of the basic psychological pitfalls that make traders fail. When a trader gets greedy, he may continue to increase his position when he is making money. Two problems arise with this philosophy. First of all, the trader may become blind to signals of an impending turnaround since he is on such a winning streak, and secondly, he may end up holding his largest position just when the market turns. A trader should never be unwilling to stop trading just in case there is more money to be made.

LAZINESS

Information is the life force of commodity trading. Identifying which information is important to the fluctuations of commodity prices and then keeping current on that information is critical to a successful trader. Being lax leads to disaster.

Much of the information surrounding commodity trading can range from useless to outright false, so the identification process is crucial. Unlike the stock market, where companies are restricted as to the information they can disseminate to the public, commodity trading thrives on rumor. Much of the information found in the literature or on the sites of trading firms is market hype, designed to attract customers to commodity trading in general and their trading platform in particular. A trader should not be too willing to follow someone else's advice (except his broker, who is being paid for it) instead of finding out the facts on his own. A good trader will make sure he has all of the factors on his side, or he will wait until they are and they can confirm his decision. A trader needs to work hard at understanding the key factor(s) motivating the market(s) he is trading. In other words, as Thomas Jefferson is supposed to have said, "I'm a great believer in luck and I find the harder I work, the more I have of it."

Each commodity is different and the factors affecting corn may not affect gold, although some economic data affects all markets. The trader has to keep on top of the relevant information for his market. The stock market strategy, where traders buy and hold a stock in the hopes of an eventual increase in value, will not work in commodities. First of all, the position will expire, and some decision has to be made before that happens or the trader will be forced to liquidate, rather than being in control of the close out of his position. Secondly, the short cyclical nature of most commodities force them to have short-term trends while the stock price of a healthy company can maintain a sustained, gradual price improvement over time.

Commodity trading is not for the faint of heart. Most successful traders cite abandoning their trading principals as the reason for most of their big losses.

ANALYZING YOUR MOVES

Anyone who wants to improve as a trader must first identify the mistakes he makes consistently and recognize the stumbling blocks he puts on his own road to success. Your losses, not your profits, will be the best teachers. Take advantage of every loss to improve your knowledge of market action. Examine the most recent losing trades and see if there is a consistent pattern. If a trading strategy and decisions were based on proven techniques, what went wrong? Too many traders see what they want to see rather than what is there. Doing an "after damage" analysis like this can be a very valuable tool, as long as you look closely and are honest with yourself. A good trader can look at things with an unprejudiced eye and see what is there, not what he wishes was there.

Another analysis technique is to look over the recent successful trades and find the ones that succeeded only by luck. It can be just as valuable to analyze successful trades as it can be to analyze losing trades. It happens frequently that a small stroke of luck is was the final determinant of a winning position. If the stroke of luck hadn't occurred, or had gone the other way, it would have been a losing trade. How would they have turned out if luck had not been on your side? Were there any mistakes with those trades that were covered up by the lucky event?

A trader's goal should not be to trade perfectly all the time, to gain on every trade, or to be perfect in any other way. Having that kind of pressure is a surefire way to make many mistakes. No one is perfect, and in trading you do not need to be perfect — you just have to consistently make more good trading decisions than bad ones. Traders who do their jobs consistently and well will outshine the ones with a few spectacular gains and many losses. A successful trader cannot afford to lose his perspective by having a few successes overshadow his many losses. The purpose of identifying stumbling blocks in your trades is not to deflate your ego. Even the best traders have weaknesses, but they realize the importance of recognizing and controlling those weaknesses.

One of the most important strategies is to develop a trading plan. As the saying goes: "You're never going to get there if you don't know where you are going." A good broker, if you work with one, will make that one of the first steps in deciding upon how his client is going to trade. The first thing to do is to choose the reason you want to get into a given trade in the first place. Let us say a novice trader has decided to enter the soybean oil market for some basic practical reasons: low margin requirements, low volatility that will allow him to watch the market closely while he learns about it, and a perceived growing demand because of health concerns with other types of fats. These are all solid basic reasons, but the trader should now supplement and support this rationale by learning about overall worldwide demand for the commodity, current crop conditions, open interest and other statistics, and studying the technical charts to see where technical resistance and support levels are. Does he want to get "paralysis by analysis"? No, but a study like this might show him that there is a glut of soybean oil and no matter how much health food enthusiasts might want to switch to it, there is more than enough supply to meet demand and the price is not going to improve much. The secret is to develop a theory and a plan, then look for factors that either support or deny it, keeping the option open to drop the theory or the plan if the factors don't support it.

MANAGING RISK

Commodity trading can be extremely risky for the same reasons that it can be extremely lucrative: the use of leverage and speed.

The bubble and crash in technical stocks taught many people about the dangers of buying stock on margin — the technique, called leverage, of borrowing money from your broker to buy stock. Recently, it has become much harder to buy stock on margin. Commodity futures, however, have long been based on margin. A trader can buy a futures contract and put down only a fraction of the total price, but if your position loses money, you have to cover the full loss. This can happen very quickly, and the real power (or danger, depending on which side of a price move you are) of leverage or buying on margin is that a small change in price can create a large change in the value of a position.

Gains and losses in futures trading are the result of price changes but this is far from the complete story. More than in any other form of speculation or investment, gains and losses in futures trading are very highly leveraged. Understanding of leverage and how it can work to a trader's advantage or disadvantage is critical to a full understanding of futures trading.

As mentioned, the leverage of futures trading stems from the fact that only a relatively small amount of money (the initial margin) is required to buy or sell a futures contract. On a particular day, a margin deposit of only $1,000 might enable you to buy or sell a futures contract covering $25,000 worth of soybeans. The smaller the margin in relation to the value of the futures contract, the greater the leverage.

If you speculate in futures contracts and the price moves in the direction you anticipated, high leverage can produce large profits in relation to your initial margin. Conversely, if prices move in the opposite direction, high leverage can produce large losses in relation to your initial margin. Leverage is a truly a double-edged sword.

While buying (or selling) a futures contract provides exactly the same dollars and cents profit potential as owning (or selling short) the actual commodities or items covered by the contract, low margin requirements sharply increase the percentage profit or loss potential. For example, it can be one thing to have the value of your portfolio of common stocks decline from $100,000 to $94,000 (a 6% loss) but quite another (at least emotionally) to deposit $6,000 as margin for a futures contract and end up losing that much or more as the result of only a 6% price decline. Therefore, it must be remembered that futures trading requires not only the necessary financial resources but also the necessary financial and emotional temperament to be able to handle such risk.

Investors who are used to the concept of margins on stock brokerage accounts will realize that buying stocks on margin really means you are borrowing 50% of the purchase price of the stock from your broker. (Stock exchange rules limit the amount an investor can borrow to 50%.) The investor pays the balance of the value stock, and owns the entire amount of stock, but pays interest on the margin borrowed from the broker. This will allow the stock market investor to have a certain degree of leverage, but neither the risk nor rewards that leverage in commodity accounts affords. At some point, the investor in the stock will pay off the margin loan with his broker, hopefully after he has sold the stock at a profit. The margin on a futures account is not a loan, but a deposit.

To visualize the concept of margins in the commodity markets, let us examine once again a trade in soybean oil, which has one of the lowest margin requirements on the exchanges. Our trader deposits an initial margin of $608 per contract to start trading, and $450 per contract as a maintenance margin. If he buys one soybean oil contract at 35.00 (35¢ per pound), he has purchased a contract worth $21,000. He is "long" the soybean oil contract, hoping the price will rise. He is right, and it increases to 36.50, and he sells, for a profit of $900 (60,000 x .355 = $21,900). His profit of $900 (less commissions and other charges) will be deposited to his margin account and he can take it out or use it for new trades. If the soybean oil market fell instead, to 33.00, his contract is only worth $19,800. This potential loss of $1,200 will count against his margin deposit, and he will have to put up an additional $142 to bring the account back to meet margin requirements and continue trading. Continual decreases in the price would require additional margin deposits until he closed out the position and took his loss. A 5.7% decrease in the price of soybean oil would cause him to lose all of his investment (margin) of $1,200.

Another major risk in commodity trading is dealing with unethical or even dishonest firms. Make sure that you research the firm thoroughly before you decide to open an account. Check on a commodity brokerage firm with the National Futures Association (NFA). NFA maintains a Background Affiliation Status Information Center (BASIC). Any investor thinking about opening a futures account should use BASIC as a resource. BASIC contains Commodity Futures Trading Commission (CFTC) registration and NFA membership information and futures-related regulatory and non-regulatory actions contributed by NFA, the CFTC and the U.S. futures exchanges. In this way, an investor can access the information on a given brokerage firm from many different agencies at the same time.

8

BUILDING STRENGTHS

"The secret of success is constancy to purpose."

— *Benjamin Disraeli*

As has been stated repeatedly, being aware of the risk, scope, and trends of the commodity futures markets is one of the primary keys to successful trading. Understanding how the so-called randomness of commodity prices works is the first step. A commodity-trading program can be developed using one of the many commodity trading systems that are available from a brokerage firm, or depending on how much the new trader is willing to invest in his trading "infrastructure," there are hundreds of software programs available to build a commodities portfolio. Finding an excellent trading system and following it consistently and for long enough for it to show results is an important factor in a successful trading career. But a new trader would be unwise to rely solely on any of these systems without a clear understanding of the basics of how to manage trades and use the tools of the market properly.

The whole system of commodity trading is based on certain logical principals.

TRENDS

Theoretical mathematicians have shown that the commodity futures market, like all financial markets, are non-linear, dynamic systems called chaos systems. Chaos systems produce random looking results without being truly random; they have a trend component that reduces the randomness of the price movements. This randomness is never completely removed, and that is why traders must accept losses along with gains, and attempt to work the odds in their favor along the trends. In other words, a trader must trade in trending markets and find pockets of opportunities along those trends. Trying to identify a certain situation that will result in an immediate price increase and yield an immediate profit is a disastrous technique in trading. Spotting and taking advantage of long-term trends is an important area to focus on. They only come a few times a year, and can be much more lucrative than short-term moves or day trading. Prices can only be watched after the fact, so commodity trading does not predict, it confirms trends.

SIMPLICITY

Prices move in certain directions based on certain forces. They have a tendency to continue moving in this direction, unless another force is introduced. A new trader entering the market should keep this tenet of simplicity in mind as he tries to understand these movements. It is simpler to consistently follow a good trading plan rather than switching from one scheme to the next. Too many unsuccessful traders will follow hot tips or use the latest trading secret being touted (and sold) instead of following a consistent, logical plan.

EXECUTION

The key to maximizing profits is how the trades are executed. How you choose to execute your commodity trades will affect overall performance of your trading system. Most commodity markets offer traders multiple platforms for execution, either the traditional open-outcry trading floor platform or a computer-based electronic platform. But most commodity system trading firms automatically route client orders to whichever platform has the lowest fees in order to save the firm dollars per trade. However, each platform has its own strengths and can be better suited for a particular market or order type. Most brokers will offer a number of different trading platforms and a trader should discuss the type of trading he will engage in so that he chooses the platform that will serve his needs best.

MANAGING EMOTION

The commodity markets are pictured as frenetic, exciting places to do business, and indeed, on the trading floors they certainly are. But in actuality, successful trading can be very boring, since a good trader will have a strategy that has been well thought out in advance, and he just follows his strategy, without being affected by the news of the day, the latest rumor, or any factor that affects his emotions instead of his strategy. It certainly is a lot more exciting to get hyped up over events and to go with a gut feeling or trade instinctually rather than systematically, and probably makes for more interesting dinner conversations. But the trader who is calm, cool, and collected and follows his plan with patience and discipline regardless of other factors is the trader who will succeed.

For futures and commodity market system trading, it is essential that these strengths are used to their fullest extent to reduce or eliminate slippage (the difference between estimated transaction costs and actual transaction costs with the difference usually composed of a price difference). Good execution and strict slippage control can make or break a commodity trading strategy.

INSTINCTS

If you are in a trade and you start to feel unsure of yourself, take your loss or protect your profit with a stop. Once you are unsure of a position, you will be unduly influenced by a multitude of extraneous and unimportant details and will probably end up taking a loss. But test your instincts to make sure they are on target. "Optimism means expecting the best, but confidence means knowing how you will handle the worst." (The Zurich Axioms) If you are only optimistic, you should avoid making a move unless you see the underlying strengths to support your market perspective. Remember, standing aside is also a position.

CUT YOUR LOSSES

The basic failing of most speculators is that they put a limit on their profits and no limit on their losses. This is why you will often see a trader let his loss run, and become larger and larger, hoping that eventually the market will turn around and prove him correct. This same principle also dictates that a trader will want to take his profit right away; this proves that he was correct. Even thought the old saying tells us that "You never go broke taking a small profit," you'll never get rich that way either, and slippage will eat up a lot of that small profit. Being satisfied with small profits is not the right mental approach for making money in speculation. If you are correct when entering a trading situation, you will know it almost immediately and will show a profit quickly. If you are wrong, you will show a loss and you should remove yourself from the situation quickly. Small losses that you incur when you exit a position that did not go as you predicted or hoped does not necessarily mean that the strategy was entirely wrong. It usually means that the timing was incorrect and that you should wait for the correct timing and situation to allow you to reenter the market.

The market is the final judge in any trading situation. No matter what a trader thinks about his trade, if he lost money on it, the market told him it was not a good trade. A trader must let the market dictate when he is wrong and when he is right. If he is showing a profit, he should let it ride until the market turns around and informs him that he is no longer right. The timing may be critical here, since a trader will want to ride the trend until it turns, but the secret is to listen to the market and get out when it does. The market will also tell traders when they are wrong and should get out and cut their losses.

SPECIALIZE

It is hard enough for one individual to fully understand and successfully trade a specific market. It is next to impossible for an individual, especially a beginner, to be successful in several markets at the same time. We have discussed over and over the importance of educating yourself and keeping on top of market information. The fundamental, technical, and psychological information necessary to trade successfully in more than a few markets is more than most people have either the time or ability to accumulate. Choose a market that is interesting to you for one reason or another and learn everything that can be learned about that market. Jumping into the "hot commodity" of the day is a sure recipe for disaster, even though there are many traders (who become part of the 94% who do not stay in the market for long) who believe they can make a killing off a tip that pork bellies are going through the roof or gold is tumbling and should be shorted.

THE TREND IS YOUR FRIEND

This is a tried-and-true maxim that all successful traders recognize and respect. It is very important that a trader be aware of this strong force in the market, whether it is bullish or bearish. When this force is at its height, it is just plain crazy to try to buck it. And do not think you only have to follow uptrends. The successful trader is not afraid to buy high and sell low. But buying on a rising market is the most comfortable way of buying, so most people prefer it. Just buy when the market is scaling up and sell when the market is scaling down. The principles of successful commodity speculation are based on the supposition that people will continue in the future to make the mistakes that they have made in the past, and this is what creates trends.

Even if a market has gotten away and you have missed the first leg, you should still consider jumping in even if it is dangerous and difficult. When it comes to commodity prices, there is never a place on a trend line when it is too high to begin buying or too low to begin selling. But after the initial transaction, avoid make a second unless the first shows a profit.

On the other hand, it is extremely important to learn to recognize when a trend is about to run its course or is near a period of exhaustion. A trader should try to developing this ability to recognize the early signs of fatigue in a given market and protect himself from staying in the market too long. Staying on top of your market and having the ability to change direction quickly when the trend changes is an invaluable skill. Know your markets well enough to recognize the factors that influence trend reversals. For instance, knowing that weather markets are inherently more volatile and can reverse quickly is important if you are holding a position in such a market. A wise trader will widen his stops so the market has plenty of room to move without taking him out prematurely. Even if you are following a trend on a chart, re-evaluate your position in the market if charts have weakened and the fundamentals have not developed as you expected or no longer support your position. The news always follows the market and so it will confirm the new direction.

NEVER ANSWER A MARGIN CALL

This simple rule will act as a stop loss when your position has weakened considerably. By consistently sticking to this rule, the market (and the margin clerk) will force you to get out of the market before disaster can strike. Nobody likes to admit they are wrong and get out of the market at a loss. But this probably should have been done well before there was a margin call, and a margin call should act as a final warning that you have let your position go as far as you logically should have. Needless to say, you should never increase your stake in a losing position.

SELL THE FIRST RALLY AND BUY THE FIRST BREAK

Another market maxim that consistently holds true. What this means is that, in general, a market which has an established trend heading either up or down will have a reaction and a trader can make good interim profits by spotting these reactions and taking advantage of them. For example, when the market is bullish, the first reaction in the market will see investors jump in who were waiting to buy the break. This kind of buying support will normally cause the market to rally. The same phenomenon will apply in a bear market: a small rally will cause many investors to cut their losses and this kind of selling further supports the fall. You don't have to be the one to predict the highs or lows. Let the market tell you when high or low has been made.

ALWAYS BE IN CONTROL

Do not allow your trading position to control you. A big key to successful trading is to know yourself and to know and understand what your hot buttons are. You should never be in a position that is larger than you can handle and you should never let a position get to this point. Large positions like this can take over emotions, feelings and good judgment. What follows is that the size of the position, instead of the trading plan, the facts of the situation and the trends of the market take over and have such a psychological impact that good judgment is suspended. Self control is easily the most important task in trading, more so even then predicting the direction of the market. You are the most important element in the success equation. Commodities do not know or care who owns them. The basic premise behind price changes is human emotion. All of the pitfalls we have previously discussed, pride, envy, greed, laziness, stress, and uncertainty are the sources of short-term price change, for that is what market participants are reacting to, but if you do not let any of them take control of you, you can beat the market because the traders who are being controlled by these outside forces are not following a plan. A trader must remain impersonal. The market is completely neutral about your losses and gains; becoming emotionally involved or upset will not change anything. Also avoid getting emotionally involved in a trade because you feel that you have invested too much time or money to give up on it and now you have to allow it enough time to show what it can do. If it is not going anywhere, move on to the next trade, stand aside and watch the market or change your plan.

Chuck Hackett, the "Pitmaster", advises us to repeatedly re-evaluate open positions. Keep asking yourself: "Would I put my money into this if it were presented to me for the first time today? Is this trade progressing toward the ending position I envisioned?" Each day brings new opportunity and developments, and your positions need to be examined against them each day.

START FRESH EACH DAY

Do not be confounded by "what ifs." If someone else entered a trade before you at 50 ticks lower, just remember this is your trade now and each day you are both going to make the same profit, regardless of how much he made before. Therefore, if the market goes up 10 ticks, you each have made the same amount that day. If the market goes down 10, you have each lost the same amount. Do not be influenced by the fact that someone has taken a position before you. Concern yourself only with your situation. Each day, start fresh. Your paper profits or losses from previous days should not enter into your decisions regarding the course of action you will take. Be able to expect and accept losses gracefully. If you have taken a loss, forget it quickly and, even more importantly, if you have taken a profit, forget it even more quickly. Do not let ego or greed interfere with your clear thinking and hard work. Those who brood over losses always miss the next opportunity.

PART II

TRADING THE COMMODITIES

In this section, we discuss basic information for each of the most widely traded commodities, including the exchange each is traded on, contract size, and price ticks. We discuss a little history and examine current factors affecting each of the major commodity groups as well as the outlook and traditional influences for each of the individual commodities.

AGRICULTURAL PRODUCTS

"I was determined to know beans."

— *Henry David Thoreau*

Agriculture is still the world's largest industry, despite the developed world's shift to manufacture or technology. On a global basis, more people are involved with farming than all other occupations combined. Today, there may be only a couple million people actively involved in "production" agriculture in the United States, but according to the International Food Information Council, one out of every six jobs is tied to the agricultural industry.

COFFEE

Coffee is the second most widely traded commodity by physical volume in the world, second only to crude oil. This seems quite appropriate, since both are usually necessary to get us to work. Coffee is said to have been first consumed in the 9th century when it was discovered in Ethiopia. It spread from there to Egypt and by the 15th century had reached Persia, Turkey and north Africa and spread across the Mediterranean to Italy and the rest of Europe. Today, coffee is one of the most popular beverages in the world.

Coffee is produced primarily in ten nations, with Brazil and Colombia being the top producers. Vietnam, Indonesia, India, Ethiopia, Mexico, Guatemala, Honduras, and Uganda are the other major producers. Coffee production is measured in bags, and one bag weighs 60 kilograms (132 pounds).

Just about the entire production of the world's coffee is made from two kinds of beans, Arabica and Robusta. Arabica accounts for 60% of the coffee beans grown in the world. It is grown both in South America and the Indian subcontinent. It is a rich tasting bean and therefore more in demand and more expensive. Its quality makes it the benchmark for all coffee prices. Robusta is the poor cousin, accounting for 40% of the world's production of beans. It is easier to grow and consequently less expensive.

OUTLOOK FOR COFFEE

Coffee has been in crisis for a number of years. Coffee has lagged behind the rest of the commodity world in the recent bull market. Coffee prices at the beginning of the 21st century were lower than prices in the 1970s. Small rallies have occurred, but the price of coffee remains low in historic terms. This has forced many formerly major coffee-exporting countries to cut production. Brazil, the largest exporter, is seeing coffee plantations converted into sugarcane and soybean fields. (The Colombian ones take the more profitable route of tearing out coffee plants to convert to the cultivation of coca, the chief ingredient in cocaine.) As growers who remain in the market continue to lose money, they have engaged in cost-cutting measures such as the reduction of the use of fertilizer or hiring less workers, both of which lower yield. Coffee is a volatile crop, requiring a lot of care and a lot of labor. The best varieties grow in high altitudes, and are subject to the vagaries of weather, especially frost. The crop is picked, sorted, and bagged by hand, a very labor-intensive commodity. Nevertheless, despite the time and amount of human intervention required to grow and process coffee, there has been an ample supply of coffee over the past decade, which is the reason for the depressed prices, even in the face of demand for coffee that increases at about 1.3% per year.

But it seems that supplies may finally have started to drop, mainly due to diversion of land and/or neglect of crops, as cited above. Combined with a weak dollar, the drop in supplies, and steady to increasing demand, the stage may finally be set for demand to outpace supply and push up prices.

Coffee trades on the Coffee, Sugar and Cocoa Exchange, a division of the New York Board of Trade. Contract size: 37,500 pounds. Price fluctuation $0.0005/lb.

COCOA

Cocoa is a seed from the cacao tree, grown in the humid areas near the equator. We all know cocoa by the most popular product it is made into, chocolate. Cocoa trade is dominated by African countries, with Ivory Coast and Ghana being the largest growers, with more production between them then between all the other exporters combined. The other growers are Indonesia, Nigeria, Brazil, Cameroon, Ecuador, Colombia, Mexico, and Papua New Guinea.

The use of cocoa increased dramatically when it was transformed from a beverage to a solid form, beginning in 1828. A method was found to press liquid cocoa butter (called liquor) out of ground cocoa beans and then used as a base with sugar to make chocolate candy. This shift from beverage to a solid added a whole new manufacturing component to the marketing chain, since it made cocoa easily transportable and very consumable. Milk chocolate, invented 40 years later, increased the attraction for chocolate since it became a smoother and sweeter product, and the demand for cocoa beans increased further. Once cocoa became available to general society, its significance in the world marketplace was secure.

The cocoa tree is a strictly tropical plant, and only thrives in hot, rainy climates located not more than 20 degrees north or south of the equator. The fruit (bean) of the cocoa tree first appears as a pod. When the pods are ripe, they are cut down and opened, and the beans are removed, fermented, and dried.

OUTLOOK FOR COCOA

Weather conditions, disease, and insects can have a major impact on annual cocoa yield, and therefore prices are subject to sudden moves. This makes cocoa futures very interesting to speculative traders who prefer commodities with sharp sudden moves. Of course, cocoa is important to hedgers such as beverage and candy manufacturers who need to protect their prices.

Cocoa trades on the Coffee, Sugar and Cocoa Exchange, a division of the New York Board of Trade. Contract size: 10 Metric tons. Price fluctuation: $1 per ton.

WHEAT

Wheat is one of the oldest agricultural products known to man, probably grown as far back as the Neolithic era. It originated in southwest Asia and was domesticated about 10,000 years ago, and throughout the centuries has been considered the "staff of life." Cultivation and repeated harvesting and sowing of the grains of wild grasses led to the selection of more resilient ears and larger grains. Although today's wheat is resilient and resistant to disease, because of the loss of seed dispersal mechanisms, domesticated wheat cannot survive in the wild.

Wheat is so widely grown, produced in over 80 countries, that no one country dominates the market. While China and India produce the most, the United States is one of the five largest producers, with the states of Kansas and North Dakota typically the leading producer states. A number of countries of the European Union are also strong producers. Russia, Canada, Australia, Pakistan, and Turkey also produce wheat in abundance. In fact, the U.S.Department of Agriculture reports that Ukraine and Russia compete directly with the United States in foreign markets for wheat in the years when their production is high. (Each year, USDA updates its 10-year projections of supply and utilization for major field crops grown in the United States, including wheat.)

The most important use for wheat is flour, the key ingredient in breads, pastas, crackers, and many other food products. Wheat byproducts are used extensively in livestock feeds, and wheat is used in many industrial applications, significantly as an ingredient in starches, adhesives, and coatings.

Japan is one of the largest importers of wheat in the world, primarily importing from Australia, Canada, and the United States. Wheat is truly a global market, permitting traders to operate in a global environment so that they can create a broad trading strategy.

OUTLOOK FOR WHEAT

Currently the U.S. wheat trading sector is facing challenges to long-term profitability. The world market for wheat is becoming stronger as domestic (U.S.) food use of wheat has declined in recent years. Changing consumer preferences, such as low-carbohydrate diets in addition to improved bread preservation technology (which means less bread thrown away) have contributed to this decline. The wheat market is fairly stable and more trend-based than many other commodity sectors, which holds a certain appeal to certain kinds of commodity investors. However, it is still important to realize that inter-market influences affect the wheat market on a continuous basis. Until just recently, U.S. wheat producers counted on rising per capita food consumption of wheat flour to continue to support domestic demand for their crop. This growing domestic consumption now appears to be at an end.

But it is important to understand the American psyche concerning wheat. The government, because of popular feelings about our domestic supply of this most basic foodstuff, supports production incentives in the U.S. and this can influence wheat production. Planting incentives are also in place; these reflect expected net returns from the marketplace. In addition, because of the seasonality of wheat prices, farmers benefit from the governmental marketing loan program when seasonal lows fall below the posted county price for wheat. When prices are low enough for marketing loan benefits, acres stay flat and trading prices are affected.

What does all of this mean? Even though wheat can be fairly stable and follow trend lines, watching the government programs, and the participation in them, can give traders some interesting opportunities for profits.

The wheat market is traded at three different exchanges:

- The Chicago Board of Trade (for soft-red winter wheat, used for cakes, pastries and cereals)

- The Kansas City Board of Trade (for hard-red winter wheat, the most important class of wheat grown in the United States, accounting for half of the wheat production. It is used as bread wheat.)

- Minneapolis Grain Exchange (for hard-red spring wheat, which is a milling quality, high-protein wheat used primarily in specialty bakery products such as croissants, French rolls, bagels, etc.)

Trading is not around the clock as in some markets, but multiple types of wheat can be traded across the country.

Contract size: 5,000 bushels. Price fluctuation: $0.0025 per bushel.

CORN

Corn is an indigenous plant of the Americas that was introduced to Europe after the colonists brought back both the seedlings and the taste for this useful grain. For centuries corn has been a staple of everyday life, used as a source of food, energy, and even monetary value. The United States grew 42 percent of the world's corn during fiscal year 2006, producing 282.3 million metric tons (11.1 billion bushels) and 80% of the production of corn in the United States comes from five Midwestern states known as the Corn Belt: Iowa, Illinois, Nebraska, Minnesota, and Indiana. Other major corn producing countries in 2006 included China, Brazil, the European Union, Mexico, Argentina, and India. The majority of corn grown in the United States is "dent" corn, so called because the kernel typically forms a dent on the cap or crown at maturity. Dent corn is used for everything from livestock feed to corn syrup and sweeteners to ethanol and industrial products. Corn, like crude oil or coffee, comes in different qualities and the most important types are High Grade Number 2 and Number 3 Yellow.

For the last ten years, corn has been the leading crop in terms of production and acreage grown. By far, the greatest use for corn is as a basis for livestock and poultry feed. But corn also serves as a main ingredient in many of the foods we eat every day, such as corn oil for margarine, cornstarch for gravy, and corn sweeteners for soft drinks. And corn is being used more and more for nonfood uses: alcohol for ethanol fuel, absorbing agents for disposable diapers, and adhesives for paper products. Corn is one of the most active of the grain contracts and this liquidity accounts for its attractiveness to speculators.

OUTLOOK FOR CORN

Because of these increasing uses, corn demand appears to be on the rise and export sales are strong. But recent erratic weather patterns are dominating the corn trade, so in addition to the usual fundamentals that affect agricultural commodities, traders are watching weather patterns with a careful eye.

Corn trades on the Chicago Board of Trade. Contract size: 5,000 bushels. Price fluctuation $0.0025 per bushel.

SOYBEANS

Soybeans, like wheat, are an ancient crop. They were first introduced into the United States in 1765, according to the Soybean Research Advisory Institute. George Washington Carver first tested soybeans, among other plants, to find uses for them and diminish the South's dependence on cotton as the single commodity of their economy. He invented soybean-based varnishes, paints, inks, mayonnaise, salad dressings, linoleum, plastic, and even fuel. Today, the world's largest producer of soybeans is the United States, dominating the market with more than 50% of the total production in the world. Until the 1980s, the United States actually produced 80% of the world's soybeans, but the 1980 grain embargo by President Carter forced the Japanese to cultivate the Brazilian soybean industry and so today South America, primarily Brazil and Argentina, is responsible for the other half of world soybean production. The majority of the cultivation of soybeans is located in the Midwestern and southern United States. Soybeans are the second most valuable crop in the United States behind corn (Soybean Research Advisory Institute), and the United States produces an average of more than 1.5 billion bushels of soybeans per year. Brazil holds a distant second place with 20% of the market, but the two nations almost completely control all of the production.

Soybeans have an incredible range of uses, and it is no wonder that they have been called a miracle crop. The most important use, of course, is as a central ingredient in many foodstuffs. They are the main ingredient in baby food, diet-food products, beer, ale, noodles, cooking oil, margarine, mayonnaise, salad dressing, shortening, etc. Lecithin, a product you see on so many products if you are a reader of product labels, is a natural emulsifier derived from soybeans. Several important low-fat sources of protein, such as tofu, miso, and soymilk also use soybeans as a major ingredient.

In addition to their value as a food product, soybeans are now being seen as a renewable resource with many industrial applications that are more environmentally friendly than traditional products. For example, many publications are printed using soy ink, which is more environmentally friendly than petrochemical-based inks. And, of course, as the pressure for finding fuel alternatives is continues, soy diesel has been discovered as a new energy source that is capturing the attention of the trucking industry. Soybeans are also used in adhesives, cleaning material, polyesters, and other textiles.

Soybean meal is derived from soybean and is the richest in protein of all the oilseeds. It is therefore used extensively for animal feed for cattle, hogs, and poultry. Soybean meal is traded as a separate contract, with a contract size of 100 short tons.

OUTLOOK FOR SOYBEANS

Export sales for soybeans are therefore strong and are expected to exceed 1 billion bushels in 2007, according to the U.S. Department of Agriculture. This is despite the fact that soybean acreage has been shifted to corn in reaction to the ethanol craze. South America may shift more acreage to soybeans in reaction to this loss of U.S. soybeans acreage in addition to the increasing demand from the biofuel sector.

Soybeans trade on the Chicago Board of Trade. Contract size: 5,000 bushels. Price fluctuation: $0.0025 per bushel.

SOYBEAN OIL

Soybean oil is extracted from soybeans. Each bushel of soybeans produces 11 pounds of soybean oil and 48 pounds of soybean meal, so the soybean oil market is very closely tied with the soybean market. It has become the most popular oil for use as a cooking oil in recent years since it contains very little saturated fat. Trading soybean oil futures is important to the food industry as it provides the foundation to stabilize often volatile soybean oil prices. Price stability is essential for those businesses that rely on soybean oil for their manufacturing processes. Soybean oil is also swiftly becoming popular as an additive in biodiesel fuels since some engines now being developed can convert from diesel to soybean oil during operation.

OUTLOOK FOR SOYBEAN OIL

Domestic inventories are at a record level, yet soybean oil prices continue to move higher. University of Illinois Extension marketing specialist Darrel Good explains: "Soybean oil prices are being supported by the global increase in biodiesel production that is consuming larger quantities of canola oil, palm oil, and soybean oil. The Census Bureau estimates that 220 million pounds of soybean oil were used for biodiesel production in the United States during March 2007. That represents 13 percent of total domestic use and exports of soybean oil during the month." Cash soybean prices (the price for the actual trading of physical soybeans) hit a marketing year high in February 2007, while it usually occurs in June or July, another indication of extreme pressure on futures prices.

Higher fossil fuel prices make it economically feasible to use the so-called green fuels. Biodiesel fuel made from soybean oil is being used more and more as an alternative to pure petroleum-based diesel. These fuels have the potential to greatly lessen our dependence on foreign oil. Biodiesel decomposes as quickly as sugar and is 10 times less toxic than salt. Investing in soybean oil looks today to be a good investment, since the need for readily biodegradable lubricants that are low in toxicity for environmentally sensitive areas has been recognized in Europe and by the U.S. government and is a research priority of the United Soybean Board (USB).

All of these factors are extremely important for potential soybean oil traders since they strengthen the futures market. However, seasonal influences run high in trading soybean oil futures contracts and consistently influence the market. Soybean oil traders must understand the critical stages of soybean oil development, as compared to trading whole soybeans. Understanding the presence of risk in the soybean oil-trading arena is important. The size and extent of risk in the soybean oil market varies greatly from year to year. However, understanding what influences the patterns may help speculators and hedgers position themselves appropriately for profit.

Risk for soybean oil trades tends to be the highest when current supplies are tight. However, in recent years when the supply has been abundant, it appears that risk premiums are not even present, most likely because of the other underlying factors. Like any trader, keep the concept or risk in mind when trading soybean oil futures, but do not expect the past to repeat itself exactly.

Soybean oil trades on the Chicago Board of Trade. Contract size: 60,000 pounds. Price fluctuation: $0.0001 per pound.

OATS

Oats found in the locations of ancient civilizations were probably weeds, and were only developed in Europe in the middle ages. They were first brought to North America along with other grains by the Pilgrims and cultivated in the New England states. By the middle of the 19th century, production had shifted to the middle and upper Mississippi valley, still a major area of production.

Oats are a staple food in many industries and world markets. The primary use for oats is animal feed (feed oats), primarily for cattle and hogs, and as any trip down the cereal aisle of your local supermarket will demonstrate, oats are also the main ingredients in many hearty breakfast foods (milling quality oats). Additionally, oats are used in the manufacture of plastics, solvents, and other industrial products. Oats are a thinner trading market than the other grain crops. The United States are net exporters of most grain crops, but oats are the only major crop that the United States imports, primarily from Scandinavia, Argentina, and Canada. Some traders consider oats as a harbinger of the feed grains markets in general, and so following oats, even if it is a market you are not interested in trading in, especially since it is a thin market, is probably a good idea if a trader has positions in other grains. The saying is "As go the oats, so go the feed grain markets."

OUTLOOK FOR OATS

For 2007-2008, world production of oats is expected to increase slightly as lower production in the United States is more than offset by higher production in the European Union, Canada, and Australia. There are two varieties of oats: milling quality used for human consumption, and feed oats for animal feed. In the United States, farmers are expected to shift some area out of oats into corn and wheat because of the recent strong demand for biofuel. U.S. production should therefore decrease causing the import demand for Canadian food oats to rise. In the European Union, production is expected to increase due to higher yields, and exports are expected to increase slightly as well. Over the medium term, prices are expected to rise on support from the rapidly expanding biofuels market. This will place further, continuous demand on corn, leading to a bullish outlook for corn, and hence oat prices are expected to remain strong, according to the Market Analysis Division of Agriculture and Agri-Food Canada. Oats are a slower moving contract in a thin market, compared to the other grains traded on the CBOT.

Oat futures are traded on the Chicago Board of Trade. Contract size: 5,000 bushels. Price fluctuation: $0.0025 per bushel, or $12.50 per contract.

BARLEY

Barley has a similar history to oats and brought to the New World by Europeans. Barley serves as a major animal feed crop, with smaller amounts used for malting beer and in health food. Today, barley is the world's fourth largest grain crop, after wheat, rice, and corn. Barley is planted in the spring in most of Europe, Canada, and the United States. Barley is hardy and drought resistant and can be grown on cropland where it is difficult to grow other crops. Barley grain, along with hay, straw, and several by-products are used for animal feed.

In 2005, it ranked fourth in quantity produced and in area of cultivation of cereal crops in the world, but this is expected to grow as barley grass powder and other derivatives from barley become more and more attractive to the booming health food market. The European Union is by far the world's largest producer of barley, accounting for 36% of world production, followed by Russia with 14% of production, and the Ukraine with 8% of production. Barley is the major feed grain in Canada, with the province of Alberta as the largest producer (Alberta produced about half of the total Canadian output of barley, 11.5-15.5 million tons, between 1995 and 2005.) U.S. planted acreage for barley has been decreasing in recent years, averaging around 5 million acres versus 7 million in the mid-1990s.

OUTLOOK FOR BARLEY

World cereal production has increased in recent years as there have been few serious climatic events in major cereal-producing areas, and productivity is continuing to improve. Australian grain production has increased significantly following several years of lower production caused by drought conditions. Global stocks have increased, putting downward pressure on world prices, although stock levels remain low in historic terms. In general, the price outlook for barley is lower than in most other commodities, which would support carrying short positions. The head of the Chinese dragon rears itself in this market as in so many others, since an important factor that will influence world prices is whether grain imports into the People's Republic of China continue to increase following years of the country stockpiling grain in an effort to be self-sufficient. In addition, the activity of futures traders is said at times to have a greater influence on the barley markets than supply and demand. There have been no significant industry developments in the coarse grain market, of which barley is a part, and the industry is composed of many small and large firms that constantly adjust to changing market conditions. It is therefore rare for major changes in this market.

Barley trades on the Winnipeg Commodity Exchange. Contract size: 20 tons. Price fluctuation: $0.10 per ton, or $2.00 per contract (in Canadian dollars).

COTTON

Cotton has been around for at least 3,500 years. The spinning jenny, spinning machine, and steam engine transformed cotton, and cotton, in turn, changed world trade. When the machine age reached the farm with the invention of a machine to separate cotton fiber from the seed, the economic power of cotton underwent another period of enormous expansion. And in the midst of the mechanization and movement of production, the boll weevil served as a reminder of the vulnerability of any crop commodity to natural disaster.

While agricultural commodities (coffee is a perfect example) are very land and climate specific, cotton can grow nearly anywhere in the world, as long as there are at least 200 frost-free days and a basic water supply. This means that the cash market (actual users of cotton) is ever shifting as conditions favor growth in different areas and technology continues to bring about dramatic improvements in the manufacture, marketing, and even genetic structure of cotton. Government involvement in pricing and production as well as international and regional trade agreements also contributes to market changes. The United States is the world's largest producer of cotton, with other major producers including China, Russia, Pakistan, Mexico, India, and Egypt. Cotton fiber is used for fabric, and cotton seed is crushed for cooking oil.

OUTLOOK FOR COTTON

Cotton futures prices are prone to sudden and dramatic moves, and therefore cotton futures are a favorite commodity to trade among individual traders and speculators. The world cotton market is one of the most volatile commodity markets there is. Of course, it is also traded as a risk-management tool for farmers and companies involved in the production and processing of cotton. Timely knowledge of these changes has been vital to those engaged in buying or selling raw cotton, and for a trader or investor interested in an exciting market with short- term moves (who is willing to do a lot of research to follow these moves), cotton can be a very lucrative investment.

Cotton is traded on the New York Commodities Exchange. Contract size: 50,000 lbs. Price fluctuation: 0.001 cent per pound, or $5.00 per contract.

ORANGE JUICE

Orange juice is the only futures contract based on a tropical fruit, oranges. Oranges are primarily grown in Brazil and the United States, but Brazil is the largest producer by far with twice the production of the United States. Other producers are India, Italy, China, Spain, Iran, Egypt, and Indonesia. The contract for orange juice is for frozen concentrated orange juice, for obvious reasons: oranges and orange juice are perishable, and since one of the criteria for commodities futures is that the underlying commodity be deliverable, they could not be traded.

Frozen concentrated orange juice (FCOJ) is a modern form of a basic agricultural commodity. Traditionally, oranges were consumed as a fresh fruit and not stored for long periods of time or easily shipped long distances, except in dried form. This changed dramatically when the process for making FCOJ was invented in Florida in 1947. Consumers demonstrated a clear preference for the convenience and taste of frozen concentrated orange juice, and they quickly substituted FCOJ for fresh oranges. Recently, the market has experienced tremendous growth internationally due to technological innovations in packaging and bulk transportation systems.

More than 70% of the oranges harvested in the U.S. are processed for orange juice. While most of the FCOJ produced in the U.S. is consumed domestically, Brazil exports most of its production. Brazil dominates this commodity world trade, accounting for as much as 80% of the FCOJ export market. Because the growing seasons of the United States and Brazil are the opposite of each other, the combined production of these two giant producers makes the FCOJ market a year-round market.

OUTLOOK FOR ORANGE JUICE

A number of factors including processing capacity, disease, and the strength of the U.S. dollar affect the supply of FCOJ. However, frozen concentrated orange juice remains a true "weather" market. Frost and freezes affect Florida production and dry weather and droughts affect Brazilian production. This sensitivity to weather factors combined with a competitive global juice/beverage market makes the price of FCOJ extremely volatile, and therefore very attractive as an investment to speculative traders.

Orange juice trades on the New York Cotton Exchange, a division of the New York Board of Trade. Contract size: 15,000 pounds. Price fluctuation: $0.0005 per pound.

SUGAR

Sugar is said to have developed in Asia, but its cultivation spread to South America via Europe and now South

America dominates the sugar trade; Brazil is the largest single producer of sugar. Other large producers are India, China, United States, Mexico, Russia, Thailand, Australia, Indonesia, and Pakistan, but sugar is produced in more than 100 countries.

There are two main types of sugar grown in the world: cane and beet. Both produce an identical refined sugar product. Sugar cane is a bamboo-like grass grown in semi-tropical regions. It accounts for about 70% of world production. Beet sugar comes from the sugar beet plant, which grows in temperate climates and accounts for the balance of production. Intemperate weather, disease, insects, soil quality, and cultivation affect both cane and beet production, as do trade agreements and price support programs.

India, Brazil, China, Thailand, Cuba, and Mexico are among the leading sugar cane producers. European Union nations, the Russian Federation, and Ukraine produce the majority of all sugar beets. The European Union, Brazil, Thailand, Australia, Cuba, and Ukraine are leading sugar exporters. Both cane and beet sugar are grown in regions of the United States; sugar beet production in the U.S. accounts for about 9% of the world total and cane production about 3% of the world supply. U.S. sugar cane is grown in Florida, Louisiana, Hawaii, Texas, and Puerto Rico. Beet sugar is grown in 14 states, with Minnesota, Idaho, North Dakota, and California leading production.

OUTLOOK FOR SUGAR

The world sugar market is expected to exceed world sugar demand by 2.3 million tons in 2007. World sugar demand has been steadily increasing over the last decade, and not just as a sweetener. The demographic impact of the "Chinese numbers" affects the sugar world as much as any other world, since China is the third largest consumer of sugar. Increased affluence and exposure to Western tastes are expected to give China a sweet tooth, creating more demand for sugar as a food product. But recently, sugar has transformed into an energy commodity, since it can be transformed (more efficiently than corn) into ethanol to power cars. More than 60% of the world's ethanol is produced from sugar. Half of Brazil's sugar crop is now used to power its cars instead of sweetening its coffee. As more and more nations commit to using ethanol fuel in order to meet the standards of the Kyoto Protocol (an agreement under which industrialized countries vowed to reduce their collective emissions of greenhouse gases), the demand for sugar will become more and more heated worldwide. Increased production of sugar is under threat as the World Trade Organization attempts to prevent the European Union from continuing the artificial support of sugar growers through subsidies. Whether this will ever happen — America outlandishly subsidizes its sugar producers as well — is a question for the future, but this places supply pressure upon a commodity that is already under significant demand pressure. The entire sugar industry closely monitors the level of sugar stocks relative to sugar consumption as a measure of available supply. In the past, small changes in the ratio have led to large price movements in the opposite direction.

Sugar has two futures contracts, Sugar #11 for world production and Sugar #14 for U.S. production.

Sugar trades on the Coffee, Sugar and Cocoa Exchange, a division of the New York Board of Trade. Contract size: 112,000 pounds. Price fluctuation: $.01 per pound.

LUMBER

Lumber is primarily traded by mills, wholesalers, homebuilders, and retail dealers so that they can manage the price risk of their most essential material and also take advantage of price opportunities. In 1969, the Chicago Mercantile Exchange became the first exchange to offer price protection to the forest products industry with the listing of random length lumber futures contracts. Lumber is primarily harvested by mills on land that is leased for its timber rights from private companies or individuals or the government. The contract specifies softwood 2 x 4s, the type used for home renovations and new home construction. The lumber futures contract traded at the CME calls for on-track mill delivery of random length 8-20 ft. nominal 2 x 4s. Primarily, the deliverable species is Western Spruce-Pine-Fir, although other Western species — such as Hem-fir, Englemann Spruce, Alpine Fir, and Lodgepole Pine — may also be delivered. Mills must be located in the states of Oregon, Washington, Idaho, Wyoming, Montana, Nevada, or California, or the Canadian provinces of British Columbia or Alberta. The acceptable grades are Standard and Better, or #1 and #2 of the structural light framing category; or construction and standard of the light framing category. Grade #2 or standard grade may not exceed 50% of the lumber delivered. Wood must be kiln dried to a moisture level of 19 percent. The random-length tally must conform to size percentage limits. Lumber of each length, for the most part, must be banded together, poly or paper wrapped and loaded on one 73' flatcar.

OUTLOOK FOR LUMBER

Traditionally, investors also like to trade lumber because it has a steady trending pattern and it is a keen indicator of the economy. But in recent years, lumber prices have reacted to supply and demand imbalances with frequent and often extreme changes. Domestic lumber supplies have been constrained for a number of reasons such as mill closings and the spotted owl controversy, along with other environmental concerns. Environmental pressure in Canada has led to the limitation of lumber supplies as the provinces move toward "sustainable" yields, where the amount of trees harvested is limited to the number that can be replaced in 40 or 50 years. On the demand side, due in part to economic conditions and interest rate policies, housing starts over the past decade have ranged from record highs to 36-year lows.

All of these factors lead to highly volatile lumber prices, which can mean opportunities for large profits. But in an industry like lumber, where costs are high and margins are tight, volatile prices also can mean risk of devastating losses.

Lumber is traded on the Chicago Mercantile Exchange. Contract size: 110,000 board feet. Price fluctuation: $.10 per 1,000 board feet or $11.00 per contract.

10

METALS

"A gold mine is a hole in the ground with a liar on top."

— *Mark Twain*

Demand for copper, silver, iron ore, aluminum, palladium, and lead continues to increase as populations grow and the demand for consumer goods increase. Yet the world has not seen one new mine shaft open in 20 years.

GOLD

Gold has a special mystique about it and has been used for centuries for adornment, money, and as an object of alchemy. Even in fairly modern times, gold was recognized as a financial standard when the world's leading countries adopted the Breton Woods Agreement in 1944 and decided to peg their currencies to the dollar, which was, in turn, pegged to gold. In 1971, Nixon canceled the dollar's convertibility to gold, an act which many people blamed for the inflationary years that followed. Gold is still used by many as a hedge against inflation and political turbulence, and trades freely like any other commodity. In addition to its magical, aesthetic, and financial applications, gold is also a very valuable commodity in the electronics industry as a semiconductor because of its conductivity properties and in dentistry because of its resistance to corrosion. Some of the important traits that have led to these uses are its indestructibility, rarity, malleability, and ductility. Malleability is its ability to be shaped into jewelry and art objects; ductility means that it can be drawn out very thinly into wire, accounting for its preferred use in electronics. Gold is one of the few commodities that can be stored and yet have its value increase over time. South Africa is the world's largest gold producer, with 25% of the world's production; Russia, the United States, Canada, Australia, and Brazil are the other major producers.

OUTLOOK FOR GOLD

Gold, according to many of the experts, may be one of the commodities that may not continue to ride the bull market. Unlike most of the futures we'll look at, where low supplies, increasing demand, and stagnating possibilities for increasing production have set the stage for skyrocketing prices, the production of gold has expanded and gold inventories are the highest they've been in history. The demand for gold for certain uses, such as jewelry, has been decreasing, although industrial demand has remained steady, and there are many who still insist on holding gold as an insurance policy against worldwide economic crises.

Gold can be invested in many forms, including gold coins, gold bars, gold certificates, and of course, gold futures.

There are two gold futures contracts that are traded: Comex gold and CBOT gold. Comex gold is traded on the Comex Division of the New York Mercantile Exchange (NYMEX) and is the most liquid gold contract in the world. It is primarily traded by the commercials such as jewelry manufacturers and mining companies for hedging. The CBOT gold contract is popular with investors and traders since it is traded in smaller sizes than Comex gold.

A Comex gold contract is 100 Troy ounces of gold, price fluctuation $10 per contract

A CBOT gold contract is 33.2 Troy ounces of gold, price fluctuation $10 per contract

PLATINUM

Platinum is used in jewelry, laboratory equipment, electrical contacts, dentistry, and automobile emissions control devices. Platinum resists wear and tarnish, which makes it ideal for crafting fine jewelry. Spanish Conquistadors supposedly discovered platinum when they were panning for Gold in Choco region of what is known today as Colombia. Considered a nuisance since it interfered with panning for gold, platinum was discarded as worthless until 1751, when a Swedish assayer, Scheffer, successfully melted and was able to work with this substance. By 1780, French glass workers were using platinum to make crucibles for glass production since it did not melt at the extreme heat used to make glass. It is this resistance to heat, corrosion, and strength that make platinum such an important industrial metal.

From its initial discovery in Colombia until 1822, South America was the world's only platinum producer. When Colombia gained its independence from Spain, it ceased exporting platinum. That did not have a major effect on the growing platinum market, since Russia was soon to replace Colombia as a supplier. Platinum was discovered in the Ural Mountains gold fields, and Russia soon became the world's supplier of platinum and is currently the world's second largest producer. Russia was also the first country to mint platinum coins, introducing this metal to the world as both an industrial and precious metal. Over 90% of the known platinum reserves in the world are concentrated in four countries.

The industrial and materialistic uses of platinum have grown over the years. In the 19th century when jewelers were able to melt platinum, "white gold" began to replace silver in jewelry. Many people prefer the lustrous white color of platinum to accentuate diamonds, and platinum bands can be much smaller since it is more than 100 times stronger than silver.

Though platinum is a relative newcomer to the industrials metals scene, it is very important to industry today. On a relative volume of annually mined metal, platinum has more industrial uses than gold and silver combined. The "rich man's gold" is sixteen times rarer than gold and generally trades at a premium to gold. Today, platinum is traded by manufacturers of jewelry, electrical and automobile equipment as a hedge against price fluctuations, but it is also traded by investors. South Africa and Russia produce 90% of the world's platinum.

OUTLOOK FOR PLATINUM

Platinum prices are expected to increase and remain steady as demand for the metal increases due to pressures to cut greenhouse gas emissions. Platinum has already gained 12% in 2007 as industrial and investment demand increased. The two main uses of platinum are in car pollution-control devices and jewelry. Auto-catalyst producers buy 54% of the metal and jewelry makers consume about 22% of platinum sold annually, according to Helen Henton, head of commodity research at London-based Standard Chartered Plc. Chidley of Barnard Jacobs also noted, "The U.S. dollar is too strong against some Asian currencies and should be weakening," increasing demand for precious metals, particularly platinum, as an alternative investment to stocks and bonds. All of this translates as very bullish news for platinum.

Platinum is traded on the Comex Division of the New York Mercantile Exchange. Contract size: 50 troy ounces. Price fluctuation: $.10 per troy ounce or $5.00 per contract.

SILVER

Like gold, silver has long been treated as a form of money as well as an important material for crafting. However, since the end of the silver standard, silver has lost its role as a common form of currency. (In 1785, the United States adopted a silver standard based on the "Spanish milled dollar." In 1861, the U.S. government suspended payment in gold and silver, effectively ending the silver standard basis for the dollar.) Now silver's primary use is in photographic paper and film for commercial photography; medical, dental, and industrial X-rays; and jewelry and electronics such as connectors, contacts and batteries. The main source of silver is in lead ore, and Mexico, Peru, and the United States are major producers of silver.

OUTLOOK FOR SILVER

Silver consumption recently has been greater than production, with current stock meeting the shortfall. This cannot continue without demand falling or production rising, therefore placing a lot of pressure on prices. Silver is one of the most volatile commodities after nickel and copper and moves very quickly and dramatically, especially in rising markets. Precious metals in general are strongly influenced by the exchange rate of the dollar, as a falling dollar makes semi-financial assets more attractive. Prospects for the dollar, which are bearish, should strengthen the silver market further in the face of the supply/demand situation.

Silver is traded on the Comex Division of the New York Mercantile Exchange. Contract size: 5,000 troy ounces. Price fluctuation: .005 per troy ounce, or $25.00 per contract.

COPPER

Copper is one of the oldest metals ever used and has been one of the important materials in the development of civilization. Because of its properties of high ductility, malleability, its thermal and electrical conductivity, and its resistance to corrosion, copper has become a major industrial metal, ranking third after iron and aluminum in terms of quantities consumed. Electrical uses of copper, including power transmission and generation, building wiring, telecommunication, and electrical and electronic products, account for about three quarters of total copper use. Building construction is the single largest market, followed by electronics and electronic products, transportation, industrial machinery, and consumer and general products. Copper directly reflects the state of the world economy. Profitable extraction of the metal depends on cost-efficient, high-volume mining techniques, and supply is sensitive to the political situation, particularly in those countries where copper mining is a government-controlled enterprise.

OUTLOOK FOR COPPER

On April 24, 2007, the International Copper Study Group (ICSG) said that its preliminary data showed that world copper production exceeded consumption by 40,000 tons in January. World mine production was up 9% from a year ago while total usage was up 6%. On May 16, 2007, the ICSG predicted that world refined copper production would exceed usage by 282,000 tons in 2007 and by 527,000 tons in 2008. The bearish threat to the copper market is usually created by Chile, where the bulk of the world's copper is produced, and Chile continues to expand production. In 2006, however, South American production was up just 1% and the biggest increase (17%) came from Africa. The growing surplus should see prices ease further, and investors in copper futures should be aware of this risk, unless they are willing to be short sellers in this market.

Copper is traded on the Comex Division of the New York Mercantile Exchange. Contract size: 25,000 pounds. Price fluctuation: 5/100 of a cent per pound, or $12.50 per contract.

ALUMINUM

Aluminum is the most abundant metal on earth, which is a good thing, since it is the second most widely used metal in the world, after iron. Aluminum provides strong but lightweight materials for building and construction, transport, consumer durables, packaging, machinery, and electrical equipment.

Despite being the most prolific metal on earth, aluminum only began to be used extensively once an inexpensive method for distilling it was discovered in the mid-19th century. It is extremely light, pliable, has high conductivity and is resistant to rust. The contract for aluminum is a very active, liquid contract, frequently representing one of four of the highest volume traded commodities.

OUTLOOK FOR ALUMINUM

Once again the developing Chinese markets are expected to have a major impact on a commodity. According to the IMF publication, World Economic Outlook (September 2006), there will be rapid growth in industrial output and construction, and the need to build and improve infrastructure in many emerging economies, which will be an engine for increased demand in the near term. However, prices have fallen 15% from at least a 19-year high in May

2006 as production outpaced demand. China is a big consumer of aluminum, but it is also the world's biggest producer of aluminum, and it is forecasting a 14% increase output in 2007.

Aluminum is traded on the London Metal Exchange. Contract size: 44,000 pounds. Price fluctuation: $.0005 per pound, or $22.00 per contract.

LEAD

Lead can be traced back to the earliest days of history. The Romans described lead as the "basest of base metals" due to the ease with which it could be beaten or melted. Lead is still predominantly used as metal and is often alloyed with other materials depending on its application. It is also used in petrol additives, pigments, chemicals, and crystal glass. But by far the biggest use of lead worldwide is the lead-acid battery, consuming approximately two thirds of the lead produced in the western world. In the early 20th century the automotive industry took off and new areas of consumption — batteries and petrol — created an enormous market. Storage batteries with lead remain, but lead-free fuels have caused a decline in usage. Because it is very soft and pliable and highly resistant to corrosion, lead was ideal for use in plumbing, but lead pipes have not been used in new domestic water supplies for about 30 years. But due to lead's corrosion resistant properties they are still used to carry corrosive chemicals at chemical plants. Ironically, environmental issues have brought about new uses for the metal, particularly in the housing of power generation units to protect against electrical charges or dangerous radiations.

OUTLOOK FOR LEAD

Lead has had a lot of bad press lately, and is no longer permitted in plumbing pipes, gasoline, and paint because of its toxic and pollutant qualities. Because of this, mine production has been decreasing, even in the face of increasing demand from lead acid storage batteries, which use more than 70% of the world's lead. This market is only going to get larger due to growing demand for cars, scooters, and trucks in the developing sectors of the world. Computers and telecommunications systems use lead, as do ammunitions, glass, ceramics, and roofing. Lead production in the United States peaked in 1999 and has been dropping since, and other large producers, such as Australia and China, have seen either unchanged or declining production.

The price of lead tripled between 1979 and 2005, and has more than doubled since mid-2005, to a near-record level of $2,070 a ton. And with environmental pressure still strong, we are not likely to see any significant increase in the production of lead to meet the increased demand. Prices for base metals in general — like copper, lead, aluminum, nickel, and zinc — have touched record highs over the past year as demand from China and India overwhelmed producers.

Lead is traded on the London Metal Exchange. Contract size: 25 metric tons, in the form of ingots. Price fluctuation: $.50 per metric ton, or $12.50 per contract.

OTHER METALS

Other metals traded include zinc, nickel, tin, and palladium. These are thinly traded compared to the commodities discussed here, and can be a dangerous area for traders, since the market for these commodities can be illiquid and not widely held. This means that often there is not someone to take the opposite side of the trade. Thinly traded commodities typically have large bid-ask spreads. In other words, a large gap exists between the price to buy and the price to sell. The wide bid-ask spread, coupled with the low trading volume, presents the problem of an trader placing an order and not getting a fill or only getting a partial fill. This can be a major problem if a position is entered and then cannot be exited because of low volume. In addition, the movements for thinly traded commodities do not offer the price movements that are attractive to investors and speculative traders. For this reason, most non-professional traders avoid these kinds of markets.

OIL AND GAS

"I don't know where speculation got such a bad name, since I know of no forward leap which was not fathered by speculation."

— John Steinbeck

During the September 11, 2001, terrorist attacks on New York, the New York Mercantile Exchange or NYMEX, where oil and gas futures contracts are traded, was destroyed, but within days the crude oil futures markets were trading again. This is a testament to the strength and viability of the energy future markets and the commodity exchanges. (NYMEX has two divisions, the NYMEX division, home to the energy, platinum and palladium markets, and the COMEX division where all other metals are traded. In addition to the NYMEX there are two other major energy exchanges: the International Petroleum Exchange of London and the Tocom of Japan. The largest by far is the New York Mercantile Exchange.)

Oil is a hot topic, with prices increasing daily and no end in sight. Oil would seem to be the classic case of a non-renewable resource that is being consumed voraciously despite the fact that it is expensive and in limited supply. There have been no major oil fields discovered for more than 35 years. Most of the extremely large reservoirs, known as giants, are well over 50 years old, and analysts believe that Saudi Arabia's oil fields may start to decline in production in just a few years. Production in the United States peaked in the 1970s and has been declining since. Not one new oil refinery has been built in the United States since 1976 and the outstanding number is declining. Many of the oil producing regions are located in unstable or unfriendly nations such as Iran, Iraq, Libya, Nigeria, Russia, and Venezuela. Add to this the predictions of America's Energy Information Administration (in its annual International Energy Outlook) that, based on today's policies, the world's consumption of energy would increase by 57% between 2004 and 2030 and that China (with the world's greatest population) will overtake America as the world's biggest energy user in the 2020s, and you have the recipe for an incredible bull market in the oil and gas sector.

CRUDE OIL, LIGHT SWEET

As dainty as the name sounds, this is the official name for petroleum or oil that is primarily used for fuel oil and gasoline. Crude oil is the largest cash commodity in the world, both in terms of dollars (over $500 billion annual turnover) and in terms of volume traded. Only money itself and its derivatives have a higher volume than crude oil. The largest producers of crude oil are Saudi Arabia, the United States, Russian, Iran, Mexico, Norway, China, and Venezuela. Not surprisingly, the United States is the largest consumer of "black gold," followed by China,

Japan, Germany, Russia, Brazil, South Korea, and India. Even though the United States is second largest producer of crude oil, it is also the largest importer. This seeming dichotomy is easily explained: the United States produces over 5 billion barrels of oil a day, but it consumes over 20 billion barrels per day, according to the Energy Information Administration. China is likewise a large producer of oil, but consumes it at a faster rate as the second largest consumer of crude oil after the United States. In the case of crude oil, many of the rules of the economics of price, supply and demand seem to go out the window. In theory, the price of a good should find its equilibrium where demand stabilizes or falls when the price of the good is too high. The other side of the equation says that production of a good should increase to meet demand when the price of the good becomes so attractive to producers. Oil is an exception in that demand continues to flourish despite continually escalating price, and production is not or cannot be increased to capture the profits from higher prices. Americans are not cutting back on their driving, and the Chinese are not cutting back on their manufacturing capacity. Meanwhile, by 2010, spare crude production capacity will have shrunk to only 1% of global demand from its current 3% level, according to Kipplinger Letters. Continually increasing demand, despite continuingly rising prices, and little to no increase in production, despite rising profit potential paint a sky's the limit scenario for the crude oil markets.

And yet, at least in the United States, there does not seem to be any great effort on the part of consumers to consume less gas. People may have become more conscious about consolidating shopping trips, and there has been a decline in sales of full sized SUVs in favor of more fuel economical cars, but Americans are still far from jumping on their bikes like the Dutch, or even driving little SMART cars, like the French. But even in Europe, total dependence on imported oil and the lack of progress in alternate fuel sources has served to maintain high oil prices.

Crude oil is traded on the New York Mercantile Exchange. Contract size: 1,000 barrels. Price fluctuation: $.01 per barrel, or $10 per contract.

HEATING OIL

Heating oil is also known as No. 2 fuel oil. The market for heating oil changed after World War II; new homes in the fifties were built with oil heaters rather than coal. In the years following the war, prices remained relatively stable because of the worldwide stability of crude oil prices at that time. In the early 1970s, this situation drastically changed when many of the governments of foreign oil producers nationalized their crude oil reserves. Following the Arab oil embargo of 1973, price stability gave way to the current volatility throughout the petroleum industry that we still see today.

When the United States lifted price controls on heating oil in the mid-1970s, the New York Mercantile Exchange began developing a heating oil futures contract and then introduced the world's first successful energy futures contract in 1978.

Heating oil accounts for almost 25% of the yield of a barrel of crude, the second largest "cut" of the barrel after gasoline, and is therefore a very important component.

In its early years, the heating oil contract attracted wholesalers and large consumers of heating oil in the New York Harbor area who were trying to hedge their use. Soon, its use spread to geographical areas outside of New York and then it came apparent that the contract was also being used to hedge diesel fuel and jet fuel, which are chemically similar to heating oil (although jet fuel is more highly refined), and therefore usually trade in the cash market at a premium that is relatively stable to heating oil futures. Heating oil was, for many years, the second most liquid energy contract after crude oil, but natural gas has shifted into this place.

Today, a wide variety of businesses, including oil refiners, wholesale marketers, heating oil retailers, trucking companies, airlines, and marine transport operators, as well as other major consumers of fuel oil, have embraced this contract as a risk management vehicle. Of course, the speculative market has equally embraced this highly liquid and volatile market (no pun intended) as a source of income from rapidly moving price shifts.

Heating oil is traded on the New York Mercantile Exchange. Contract size: 42,000 gallons. Price fluctuation: $.01 per gallon, or $420 per contract.

UNLEADED GASOLINE

Unleaded gasoline has been in high demand recently, so the price of unleaded gasoline has been soaring, while the capacity to produce it has diminished. Over the last quarter century, the number of refineries in the United

States has dropped to 149, less than half the number that existed in 1981. But because companies have upgraded and expanded these operations, refining capacity has only shrunk 10 percent during this time (from a peak of about 18.6 million barrels a day). Domestic refining capacity is expected to grow only by 0.8 percent according to Jacques Rousseau, an oil analyst with the investment banker Friedman, Billings, Ramsey. Gasoline accounts for nearly half the crude oil consumed in the United States, clearly a case of demand exceeding supply.

Unleaded gasoline is traded on the New York Mercantile Exchange. Contract size: 42,000 gallons. Price fluctuation: $.01 per gallon, or $420 per contract.

NATURAL GAS

Natural gas production has likewise lagged behind demand for at least ten years, and gas deposits around the world are declining in production. There have been new deposits discovered, but usually they are deeper deposits that are more difficult and more expensive to extract. The gas fields in Canada and Alaska are easier to exploit, but do not have the necessary pipelines to bring the product to the customer. Today, environmental pressure makes it difficult to gain permits for new wells and even when permits are granted, they are very restrictive and consequently limit the operating capacity of the wells. Even though the U.S. government is currently encouraging the building of new natural gas terminals, opposition from environmentalists makes such building difficult. Natural gas is, like home heating oil, strongly influenced by weather-related usage. Recent cold winters in the northeast have been responsible for a rise in total natural gas consumption in 2007, up more than 10% in the first quarter of 2007 compared with the same period in 2006. In annual terms, natural gas consumption is expected to rise by 3.4% in 2007 and by 0.9% in 2008.

Natural gas production has increased by 1.3% in the first quarter of 2007, but clearly production is not increasing at the levels of consumption. Projections are for increases of only 0.9% in 2007 and 1.4 % in 2008. Higher U.S. prices relative to those in other countries contribute to a surge in imports and should continue to drive growth in the near term. Natural gas is the second most actively traded energy contract, after crude oil, overtaking heating oil.

Natural gas is traded on the New York Mercantile Exchange. Contract size: 10,000 million British Thermal Units (MMBtu). Price fluctuation: $.01 per gallon, or $420 per contract.

OUTLOOK FOR OILS

Whether deciding to trade crude oil or any of its derivatives, or the spread between them, these are not markets for the faint of heart. Prices of crude oil futures continue to escalate and it sometimes seems that there is no end in sight. Even in the face of what seems to be inevitably increasing prices, the slightest news can put even further pressure on this upward spiral. Events such as refinery closings due to weather or repair, tight inventories, high travel periods, increases or decreases in crude oil stockpiles, hurricanes in the refinery regions and cyclones in the production regions, can all trigger a market which is already about as jittery as a market can be. Unless real, sustainable progress can be made in alternative fuel sources, or the world appetite for petroleum slows down (a very unlikely event given the projected growth in the developing world), traders are probably looking at a steadily uptrending market.

MEATS

"The symbol of all relationships among...men, the moral symbol of respect for human beings, is the trader."

— *Ayn Rand*

LIVE CATTLE & FEEDER CATTLE

Some historians believe that cows were the first domesticated animal. In many societies, they are the most valuable asset of the household, producing goods vastly out of proportion to their low maintenance costs. They eat grass, which is widely available and, in turn, give their owners milk, cheese, yogurt and, ultimately, meat and leather.

In 1964 the Chicago Mercantile Exchange introduced a futures contract on live cattle. In addition to live cattle futures, live hog futures were added in 1966, and feeder cattle were added in 1971. In 1997, lean hog futures and options replaced the live hog contracts. In 1999, stocker cattle futures and options were added.

These were very innovative moves, since futures up until that time were only traded on storable commodities such as grain. But the Merc recognized that the livestock industry was as ready as any of the other commodity markets for a central futures market and the advantages trading futures could bring to the industry. Live cattle and feeder cattle futures have enabled cattle producers to manage their price risk more effectively.

The United States is the largest producer and consumer of beef, but cattle are raised all over the world. The grade of beef that is traded in the futures market is used almost exclusively for human consumption. Live cattle are raised as calves with their mothers until they are weaned and then they are placed in a "backgrounding" operation. Here, they are fed grass, wheat, or other roughage until they reach the feedlot weight of 600 to 800 pounds and then they are considered feeder cattle. Since the contract for feeder cattle is 50,000 pounds, each contract represents about 60 cows. At this point, they remain in a feedlot until they are 1,000 to 1,300 pounds and are considered ready for slaughter. Different grades of beef are bought by restaurants, schools, hospitals, and for household use. Once the edible portion of the beef has been used, the remaining parts of the cattle are used in the production of leather, soaps, animal feed, camera film, and a variety of other products.

Just as in any basic commodity market, livestock producers face a great deal of risk, but the risks are different and more varied. Weather, which affects feed costs, is an uncertain factor in just about any of the futures markets, but livestock producers also face the availability of feed and forage, rates of gain of the livestock, conception rates, survivability of young animals, risks of disease, and changes in shipment rates. Another risk is the constant threat of disease.

Demand for beef fluctuates wildly. A big factor that affects demand is personal income. The more money people make, the more they are willing to pay for a steak at a good restaurant, or even to put on the grill. Higher income and standard of living usually translate into increased demand for high-quality beef faster than for most other foods. If people are tightening their belts, however, fancy cuts of beef are the first thing to go. The general public's diet preferences also have a profound effect on demand for beef and therefore price. The mad cow disease scare pushed some people away from beef. More recently, diet fads like Atkins have brought people back to beef consumption.

But this does not address their market risks, and the producers use the futures market to manage this risk. Because of the large number of market risks in this commodity, the contract can be fairly volatile and therefore is an attractive vehicle for speculators. Speculators in the livestock market serve the same purpose as in other markets: to offer liquidity to the hedgers while they try to make a profit for themselves. Most people will remember the famous case of Hillary Clinton, who, before she became First Lady, was able to parlay a $1,000 margin deposit into nearly $100,000 profit on the livestock market. She supposedly had expert advice and did a lot of research on her own, but it was viewed at the time as a very unusual experience for a first-time trader, especially since she made the profit by shorting the market, which is not typical for a novice investor. But it does point out the amazing profit potential in these markets.

OUTLOOK FOR CATTLE

Commodity prices have a tendency to affect each other in many ways and in many markets, but none so much as the livestock market with the feed grains market. If demand for beef does not increase while the costs of feed continue to do so, breeders profit margins are severely squeezed. Overall live cattle demand is being propped up by decent beef exports and a bit smaller beef imports, but 2006 demand for beef by the U.S. consumer was down 0.8% from a year earlier according to Ron Plain from the University of Missouri. If these kinds of trends continue, the outlook for cattle will be bearish.

Also known as livestock, live cattle and feeder cattle are traded on the Chicago Mercantile Exchange. Contract size: 40,000 pounds of steer averaging 1,100 to 1,300 pounds each. Price fluctuation: $.00025 per pound, or $10.00 per contract.

LEAN HOGS

Lean hogs are a fairly new addition to the Chicago Mercantile Exchange, having been launched in 1997 when the live hog futures contract was retired since this contract did not reflect the actual product in the cash market. Hogs stay on the farm on which they were born from birth to delivery. In the lean hog market, hogs of the proper weight, 220 to 240 pounds, are brought to market, and the hog is slaughtered. About 20% of the meat goes towards ham and approximately 17% of it is destined to be used as pork loins. The belly of the hog, which is cured and sliced to produce bacon; accounts for another 15% of the carcass weight.

The lean hog contact is not very liquid because it is used primarily as a hedging tool by commercial producers of pork products.

Hogs are traded on the Chicago Mercantile Exchange. Contract size: 40,000 pounds of lean value hog carcasses. Price fluctuation: $.00025 per pound, or $10 per contract.

PORK BELLIES

The Chicago Mercantile Exchange began trading frozen pork belly futures in 1961 — the first futures contract based on frozen, stored meats. Trading in frozen pork belly contracts was developed as a risk management tool to meet the needs of meat packers who processed pork and had to contend with volatile hog prices, as well as price risks on processed products held in inventory. This futures contract was designed to help processors and warehouse operators manage these price risks.

Pork bellies are the cured carcass of a slaughtered pig and account for roughly 15% of the carcass weight of the hog. The belly is cured in a heavy, salty brine solution and put in cold storage and is eventually sliced into bacon. Bacon, the end result of the pork belly, is unique among meat products in that it has no real substitute, although turkey bacon is making some inroads into the market. The major factors affecting pork belly prices are the number of hogs being slaughtered and the demand for bacon. Pork bellies are a seasonal market, and an inventory buildup typically takes place in the beginning of the year, resulting in lower prices, and then shifts to a supply-side basis that pushes prices back up, but both of these are tempered by consumer demand. Pork bellies futures are known as a very volatile, erratic market and consequently attract more speculative interest than most other contracts. Demand for bacon is waning along with demand for other high-fat, high-cholesterol foods as the American diet becomes more health conscious. This cyclicality of this product results in one of the most extremely volatile futures market.

Pork bellies are traded on the Chicago Mercantile Exchange. Contract size: 40,000 pounds. Price fluctuation: $.01 per pound, or $400 per contract.

13

CURRENCIES & FINANCIAL INSTRUMENTS

"There have been three great inventions since the beginning of time: the fire, the wheel, and central banking."

—*Will Rogers*

The highest volume futures market is not the physical commodities markets we have been discussing, such as agriculturals, metals and oils, but rather the financial futures markets. The financial futures markets include interest rate futures, foreign exchange futures, and stock index futures. Each of these markets is influenced by roughly the same factors, and they also influence each other. Interest rates, for instance, have a strong influence on the stock market and currencies; stock markets influence interest rates since the demand for a currency will be influenced by demand for the corporate stocks of that country.

Financial futures are contracts based on underlying financial instruments. These can be interest-rate sensitive instruments such as U.S. Treasury bonds, equity instruments such as the Standard & Poor's 500 Index, or currencies such as the Euro.

Like all futures contracts, a financial futures contract specifies a specific quantity of the underlying financial instrument at a market-determined price. They can be settled via cash or physical delivery, depending on the instrument. Just as with physical commodities, supply and demand factors determine pricing, and while common fundamentals often influence many markets globally, there are also factors that are unique to each particular market. And, like other commodity futures markets, traders in the financial futures markets make full use of the entire spectrum of technical trading tools.

Financial futures were developed amid a rapidly growing trend toward globalization in the world's investment and economic environment starting in the early 1970s. They were designed to meet new needs and risks that businesses, governments, and individuals faced with rapidly changing capital flows. Even though their history is much shorter than agricultural futures, they now dominate exchange-traded instruments. Today, the majority of futures traded globally are financial-based contracts, and futures exchanges are continually on the lookout for new products to add to this category.

INTEREST RATE FUTURES

Interest rates are, effectively, the price of money. Like the prices of all other goods and services, interest rates (the price of money) are determined primarily by supply and demand. Barring any influences that might counteract the normal behavior of interest rates, an increased demand for money will drive up the price of money, i.e., the interest rate. What influences the demand for money? This demand is influenced by many factors: the underlying economic health of the country, the level of government borrowing, the current rate of inflation, as well as the perception or expectation of future inflation, demand (or lack of demand) for a nation's goods, which is measured in its balance of trade. These fundamental factors are further influenced by the actions of the country's central bank. A nation's central bank can purposefully manipulate interest rates: adjust them upward in an attempt to slow the economy, or adjust them downward when they perceive that the economy is in need of stimulus.

The interest rate futures products that are traded on the financial futures markets include short-term instruments, such as the Federal funds rate and the overnight inter-bank lending rate, as well as long-term instruments such as the 30-year Treasury bond. The relationship between short- and long-term interest rates is called the yield curve. The interest rate on a given financial instrument is referred to as its "yield". As a general rule, the yield curve has an upward slope, since longer periods of lending risk will result in higher rates for longer term instruments. In other words, the longer the term of the underlying financial instrument, the higher the interest rate will be. The rationale behind this is that investors have to be compensated for being willing to lock in their investment for a longer time at a fixed rate. It can happen that the yield curve is inverted, that is, the interest rate on longer term instruments is lower than that on shorter term ones. This is most frequently caused by market perceptions that short term interest rates are artificially high and that they are destined to fall. Consistent, strongly inverted yield curves have usually presaged economic downturns.

The yield curve moves on a daily basis, a fact that is taken advantage of by financial futures markets players to "arbitrage" this fluctuation, that is, buy and sell the short and long term interest rate instruments against each other to take advantage of temporary aberrations.

EURODOLLAR FUTURES

Eurodollars are U.S. dollars on deposit in commercial banks outside the United States, primarily in Europe. Eurodollars are used to settle international commercial transactions and are not guaranteed by any government, but rather by the obligation of the bank that holds them. Eurodollar futures are based on the London interbank offered rate (LIBOR) for a 90-day, one million dollar deposit, and is today the most actively traded futures contract in the world.

The Eurodollar future contract is traded on the Chicago Mercantile Exchange on the GLOBEX electronic platform and represent the LIBOR rate for a three-month, $1 million offshore deposit. This is the same concept of standardization that is reflected in any other commodity, that is, that a trader understands exactly what instrument he is buying or selling. Just as a soybean trader knows he is dealing in 5,000 bushels of soybeans with each contract he trades, the financial futures trader knows that he is buying or selling a three-month, $1 million offshore deposit. The CME lists 40 quarterly futures contracts, spanning 10 years, plus the four nearest serial (nonquarterly) months. The Eurodollar contract is viewed as a barometer for monetary policy implications; its yield is very closely tied to the Federal funds rate. Therefore, any economic statistics that may have an effect on monetary policy will have a big influence on Eurodollar futures prices as well.

TREASURY FUTURES

The United States government has never defaulted on its debt. Because of the stability of U.S. government debt that this illustrates, treasury instruments of the United States are often referred to as "safe-haven" investments. As a rule, when global or economic shocks reverberate in the financial markets, there is strong buying of U. S. Treasury futures. This action in the market is often referred to as a "flight to quality" by investors. On the other hand, any loss of confidence in the U.S. government, inflationary tendencies that surface, or any unpopular actions by the Federal Reserve Bank will result in strong sales of treasury futures.

Treasury futures are the derivatives that track the prices of specific treasury securities. The three traded Treasury Futures are U.S. Treasury bonds, U.S. Treasury notes, and U.S. Treasury bills.

U.S. Treasury bonds are long-term debt issues of the U.S. government with maturities of more than 10 years. The "long bond", or the thirty year bond was, for many years, considered a benchmark indicating the market interest rates in general. But as the U.S. government issued less and less of them, they are less of an interest rate indicator than they once were. Today, the ten-year note is considered a more reliable benchmark.

U.S. Treasury notes are medium-term obligations of the U.S. government with maturities that range from one to 10 years. The most actively traded notes are the two-, five- and 10-year Treasury notes.

Treasury bills are U.S. government debt issues with maturities of up to one year. Treasury bill, or T-bills are the most widely issued government debt security; they are auctioned weekly and monthly. The T-bill interest rate is one of the most indicative barometers of the risk-free rate of variable return to investors. Because of their short durations, T-bills are considered money-market instruments, even outside of the futures markets. Treasury bills, bonds and notes do not pay interest. Instead, they are sold at a discount from their face value, and upon maturity, the investor receives the face value. The difference between the face value and the price at which it was sold is treated as interest.

The strength of the American economy, inflation (or inflation forecasts) and monetary policy are the major influences on how the prices of Treasury futures move. Demand for money in a strong economy or an economy that is experiencing inflationary tendencies typically causes cash Treasury yields (the interest rate paid on the underlying instrument) to rise and the price of the futures to fall, while conversely, a weak economy will usually cause yields to fall and futures prices to rise. This is how any company or organization that is exposed to interest rate risk can have the ability to offset, or hedge that exposure. For example, frequently insurance companies that have annuities payable at a fixed interest rate will sell treasury futures. If interest rates go up, they buy the futures at a lower price and therefore make a profit to offset their higher cost of funds. (Once again, the concept operates in the same manner that non-interest rate futures trading does. The soybean farmer may get less for his crop, but if he buys soybean futures to offset his sale of physical soybeans, he will profit on his futures, or hedge position, the lower price he will pay for his long soybean futures position will offset the loss.)

FOREIGN GOVERNMENT DEBT FUTURES

Foreign governments issue short and long term debt, just as the United States government does, and so many have corresponding futures contracts listed at exchanges all over the world . The largest futures exchanges for these types of financial futures, Eurex and Euronext. liffe, trade a broad range of international bench mark products, including euro-bund futures, which are long-term debt instruments, and three-month euribor futures, which are short-term instruments.

Before the European Monetary Union was introduced in 1999, German government bonds were the recognized benchmark for the European government bond market based on their liquidity, credit rating, and a record of stable German monetary policy as well as Germany's market size and depth. Among issuers of government debt in Europe,

Germany had been the U.S. equivalent of a "safe haven" for the Euro area. The integration of Europe's markets with the EMU, however, has created new debt instruments with other and different market influences.

In the U.S., the Chicago Board of Trade lists futures on three German debt instruments-Euro Bund futures (based on short-, medium- or long term debt instruments issued by the Federal Republic of Germany or the Swiss Confederation with remaining terms of maturity of 8 ½- 10 ½ years), Euro Bobl futures (based on short- and medium- term debt with remaining terms of maturity of 4 ½ -5 ½ years) and Euro Schatz futures (based on short- and medium- term debt instruments issued by the Federal Republic of Germany or the Swiss Confederation with remaining terms of maturity of 1 ¾ to 2 ¼ years). Contract values are $100,000 or CHF100,000. These contracts trade exclusively on the CBOT's electronic platform.

SWAP FUTURES

Swaps are agreements between two parties to exchange periodic interest payments. Interest rate swaps have been in existence for decades as a means for two different parties to establish an interest rate exposure that most closely matches their business or commercial needs. They are frequently used by hedgers and speculators to manage maturities of fixed or floating debt instruments. Interest rate swaps can be fixed for fixed, fixed for floating, or floating for floating, and the legs of the swap can be in the same currency or different currencies. The outstanding amount as of December 2006 was $229.8 trillion, according to the Bank for International Settlements, which reports it as the largest component of the OTC (over the counter) derivatives market. According to the Chicago Mercantile Exchange, these contracts are ideal for hedging cash market interest rate swaps while offering an innovative product that could be spread against CME's highly liquid Eurodollar futures and options contracts. Because of these factors, they have become an interest rate benchmark and are an innovative means for those seeking ways to transfer financial risk, according to the CME. Swap futures are traded at the Chicago Mercantile Exchange and Chicago Board of Trade to allow investors involved in U.S. dollar-denominated swaps to take advantage of new trading and hedging opportunities. Investors trade two-year, five-year and 10-year swap futures, in contract sizes of $500,000, $200,000 and $100,000 respectively.

CURRENCY FUTURES

Currency futures are also known as foreign exchange, forex or simply FX. Financial institutions, investment managers, corporations and private investors all trade currency futures to manage their risks and capture profit opportunities associated with currency rate fluctuations. Any company that trades globally, any investor who holds a security or position that is dominated in a currency other than his own and every bank that has international settlements all have currency risk exposure, and they will attempt to mitigate that risk by using currency futures.

Trading currencies is always two sided. On international exchanges, the opposite side of any commodity futures contract is usually the U.S. Dollar: if your commodity position goes down in price, you will have to exchange dollars to cover it and if it goes up you will gain dollars to reflect the profit. In dealing in currencies, you don't actually trade one currency but a pair based on its relationship to another currency, so the opposite side of the trade is the other currency. Since two different currencies are always involved, many factors affect the trade because the relative strength or weakness of one currency vs. another is at the heart of the trade. In effect, it usually comes down to comparing one nation's economy to another's. In general terms, healthy, expanding economies have stronger currencies and recessionary economies have weaker currencies. The factors that influence a currency's value include gross domestic product (GDP), the trade balance between countries, the interest rate on each currency and the inflation rate of the currency's country. The current account balance and money flows from one country to another reflect a currency's supply and demand, which determines the price, or exchange rate of the currency. Traders are always watching each country's trade balance to see changes in surpluses/deficits that will affect the exchange rate. Other factors influencing currency valuations include fiscal and monetary policies, including interest rates on government-issued securities, and, of course, the general political climate. The currencies of more stable economies will be stronger than those of more volatile ones, even taking interest rate and trade balance factors into account.

The currency market (or Forex market or foreign exchange market) is a world wide market, where the currency of one country is exchanged for the currency of another country. The currency market doesn't trade in any fixed location and therefore, by its nature can be defined as an over the counter market (OTC markets). The Forex market is basically just a huge network of currency dealers who are connected with each other via telecommunication facilities, and which therefore functions as a single market 24 hours a day. Open positions may be passed from trading desk to trading desk around the world; a position taken in New York on one day may be handed over to brokers in Los Angeles, Tokyo and London before it is settled. Currencies were actually the first financial futures contracts that were ever traded. The spot and forward markets in currencies are much bigger than the futures markets in currencies, but this market is dominated by banks, including government central banks.

The Chicago Mercantile Exchange is the leader for currency futures trading in the United States, and offers a variety of contracts with pricing based on a nation's respective currency value vs. the U.S. dollar. At the CME, traders have the possibility to access cross-rate futures contracts, even though most currencies are settled against the U.S. dollar. Cross-rate futures allow a value comparison of a currency against another currency besides the U.S. dollar. For example, you can trade futures on the Australian dollar vs. the Canadian dollar on the CME.

The main currencies, which have the largest share of trading in the currency markets are the U.S. dollar (USD), the euro (EUR), the Japanese yen (JPY), the Swiss franc (CHF) and the English pound sterling (GBP). Each currency pair has its own requirements.

The currency market operates 24 hours a day, five days a week, except for national holidays. There are institutions in each time zone that buy and sell currencies during the entire working day. The currency market opens at 00:00 (GMT) on Monday and closes at 0:00 on Saturday. This kind of continuous operation, not surprisingly, makes the currency market an attractive vehicle for investors and speculative traders.

Another important feature that contributes to the popularity of the currency markets among investors and speculators is that it has very large leverage ratios. A leverage ratio of 1 to 100 in the currency markets permits transactions in amounts hundreds of times higher than the original deposit. The daily rate fluctuations, also known as the volatility, in the currency exchanges can be between 150 and 250 points on an average day. Thus, each day there is a possibility of earning between $1,500 and $2,500 from every contract bought or sold. In addition, more volatile fluctuations may occur when central bank intervention occurs, or if there is significant business or political news. Fluctuation may decrease when certain events have been anticipated and it is said that the market has discounted an event or some other kinds of news. For example, if the Federal Reserve Bank in the United States is expected to maintain interest rates at the current level, and then, at their Tuesday meeting, they do just that, there will be little to no impact on the currency markets. If their actions take the market by surprise, of course, that will be a completely different story.

Despite all of this potential volatility, when currency positions are well managed, the currency markets offer the most profit potential with the least margin requirements of any of the similar markets.

According to the historian Paul Kennedy, author of Preparing for the Twenty-First Century, the amounts traded and exchanged in the international currency markets now surpass trade in manufactured goods between nations. The Bank of International Settlements estimates that $1.5 trillion moves around the world between the banks and trading houses that process these transactions on a daily basis. Recently, currency markets have become even more international, as more and more changes in the banking and securities industries occur. Banking deregulation has been on the increase in both the United States and Europe and this has allowed new players to enter this arena. Deregulation consolidates the markets across national borders but it also increases transactions both by promoting competition between the players and by giving all financial services new areas in which to operate. Both the large traders and small trading houses all compete for this lucrative and popular investment and speculative vehicle. Mergers such as that of the HSBC Bank (formally known as Hong Kong and Shanghai Banking Corporation) with the United States based Merrill-Lynch, and Switzerland's Union Bank of Switzerland with the United States based Paine-Webber mean that bank customers can easily become traders and avail themselves of just about any financial service at one location or with one call. They can access financial services, currencies (further fueling the growth of this market), brokerage services, etc. At the same time, there has been a rise in the number of affluent people who have high disposable incomes and can easily access the technological facilities that allow them to use a wide range of financial instruments. They are more computer savvy as well as more investment savvy and are willing to step into new markets to meet their investment goals or add diversity to their portfolios. This new investor/trader can easily switch between the kinds of instrument he trades and where he trades it, which further increase the demand for currencies and other financial instruments.

This dramatic growth in personal trading coupled with the ability to manage wealth globally has led to a dramatic increase in the financial futures markets. A clear indication of this is that, even though the volume of foreign currency trading has increased dramatically in recent years, the amount involved in each transaction has actually declined. A lot more players in this market mean that there will no longer be the major players who can unduly influence the market as in the past. These new developments make it doubtful that the dramatic disruptions that occurred in the foreign exchange markets in the past, such as the actions of George Soros, could occur today.

In addition to these kinds of systemic changes in the currencies markets, the introduction of the Euro has had a dramatic effect on currencies markets. The Euro is the currency for 13 of the 15 members of the European Union. With all of the traditional European national currencies no longer in play, European traders increasingly look elsewhere for currency deals. The European Central Bank forecasts increasing competition in the Euro-dollar and Euro-yen markets, "with a consequent narrowing of margins and a decline in fees." Traditionally, Europeans do not participate in the securities markets to the same extent that Americans do: only 5–10% of Europeans own stocks, compared to 30% of Americans. But Europeans do tend to be more actively involved in international markets, which require foreign currencies.

The most actively traded futures contracts are the Euro (contract size $125,000), the Yen (contract size ¥12,500,000), the Swiss Franc (contract size CHF125, 000), the British Pound (contract size £62,500), the Dollar (contract size $1,000 index) and the Canadian Dollar (contract size C$100,000). Other foreign exchange futures contracts that are traded, but to a much smaller extent than the Euro, Swiss Franc, Pound and Dollar are: the Mexican Peso, the Australian dollar, the New Zealand dollar, the South African rand, the Russian ruble, and some Asian currencies. The only reason the Chinese Yuan is not on this list is because the Chinese government does not allow it to be traded freely.

The major operators in the currency markets include hedgers, just as in any other commodities market. The difference is that just about everyone has an exposure to money and so companies that trade globally have foreign exchange risk on top of any other risk in their basic market. In other words, a European company may have an exposure in gold or oil, but since their assets are denominated in the Euro, they have the added foreign exchange risk. This risk represents a potential depreciation or appreciation in value of the currency held or required. If a producer is to receive funds in a foreign currency, he may fix his price on his goods based on the current exchange rate. If the value of the currency he is to receive falls, he will lose money. Of course, if the value increases, he will make more money, but most manufacturers and producers are interested in protecting the profit they have on their products by buying or selling the foreign exchange futures and locking in a cost. Many factors influence the value of currencies, but the major ones are:

Interest Rates. Interest rates that are higher in one country than another will induce investors to buy securities or other interest earning instruments of that country. This will create demand for the currency of that country, thereby raising its foreign exchange rate. Money flies around the world in response to changes in interest rates. If the interest rate on government bonds in a Euro denominated currency, for example, is lower than the rate on an equivalent government bond in the United States, then money should flow into dollars and out of Euros to buy those bonds (assuming no other factors have a more significant impact). The major factors that, in turn, affect interest rates are the unemployment rate, which is an indicator of the strength of the economy; the inflation rate; the price of gold and oil which are indicators of upcoming inflation; housing starts, another indicator of both the economy and the demand for money; business statistics such as industrial production; business inventories; retail sales and car sales; and government statistics such as the Gross Domestic Product, money supply, balance of trade, and the index of leading indicators.

Since the single most important influence on interest rates is the decision by the Federal Reserve Bank to increase or lower the discount rate, the actions and decisions taken at the Federal Reserve's Open Market Committee meeting, which occurs monthly, should be closely watched. (The central banks of other countries, including the European Central Bank, which controls the interest rates on the Euro, have a similar system, and changes by those central banks will affect other currencies as well as their own currency.) The Fed also influences the interest rate market by buying or selling repos (repurchase agreements) to add or decrease reserves to the system, or by intervening in the interbank market by buying or selling government securities and thereby influencing the fed funds rate, which is the rate banks lend money to each other.

Inflation Rates. Even if the interest rate of a country is high in "nominal terms" (the actual interest rate), it may not be as high in "real terms" (the interest rate adjusted for inflation). A high interest rate on a security you invest in will be worthless if inflation is high and the value of that security erodes. The inflation and the inflationary expectations in each country will affect currency values.

Supply and Demand. If a country's products sell at a lower price than another country's, buyers will want to buy those products. Importers will have to buy that country's currency in order to obtain and market those products. This will increase the demand for that currency and therefore its foreign exchange rate. However, as the exchange rate increases, the country's products will become more expensive to outside markets, and demand for the product, and the currency, will decrease, lowering the exchange rate.

Relative Income. This wealth effect allows domestic consumers to buy more and more consumer goods from other nations. This increases demand for other currencies, and lowers the exchange rate of the domestic currency. This is also reflected on a national level, since the country's reserves (gold, cash, foreign exchange reserves, or its natural resources) affect its ability to pay down loans, finance imports, and make investments and therefore increase demand for its currency.

The Stock Market. As an alternative investment to currencies and other financial futures, investing in the stock market (directly by buying corporate stocks, or indirectly by buying mutual funds) has traditionally had a strong influence on financial futures. The stock market, in turn, is influenced by many of the same factors that drive commodity markets, but frequently in different ways or in different cycles. General economic activity, interest rates, inflation or inflationary expectations, political factors, investor attitudes, and many, many other issues (actually almost any issue) can see a reaction in the stock market. Watching the stock market is important for a trader of any commodity because of the correlations discussed in Chapter Three, but it is especially important for a trader of financial futures.

Economics and Politics. The trade balance of a country has a major impact on the value of the currency. The trade balance is the difference between the amount of goods a country imports and the amount it exports. If it imports more than it exports, it will have a trade deficit and if it exports more than it imports it will have a trade surplus. A greater trade deficit will weaken the currency of a country because it needs to buy more of other currencies in order to pay for these additional goods.

Intervention on the part of the central bank of a country can have a major impact upon the foreign exchange markets. Countries will frequently, alone or in concert with other countries, support or weaken their currency in order to achieve monetary or trade balance related goals. These interventions can have a vast impact on the currencies markets, but the large speculative operation in currencies can also be a counterbalancing influence.

A country's economic policies can greatly affect the potential for investment and therefore demand for its currency. An unstable economic policy, especially one that has resulted in default on its debt, will discourage foreign investors from buying that country's securities, and consequently, its currency. An unstable political environment will likewise discourage investment. If a country is able to maintain a stable monetary policy, leading to low inflation and higher real interest rates, investors will be attracted to it. A stable political environment encourages investment.

All of these fundamental factors force the prices of currencies (the exchange rate) up and down constantly. Sometimes one factor will offset another, causing moderate moves in the exchange rate; sometimes several factors will work in conjunction, causing major currency swings. Frequently, central banks will intervene to stabilize the currency of their own country, or a group of central banks may act in consort to support another currency.

You can scarcely discuss commodity trading without discussing the famous Chinese influence. We have discussed how increasing growth and demand in China has had such powerful influences over the prices of oil, metals and other commodities, and the financials are far from immune to this influence. China is a major trade surplus country. China's trade surplus will reach $250–$300 billion in 2007, driven by the country's price competitiveness and strong external demand, the top economic planner said in June of 2007. China's surplus hit a record $177.5 billion in 2006. In the first four months of 2007 the surplus totaled $63.3 billion, up 88 percent from a year ago. (WorldNews report, June 11, 2007). China has over a trillion dollars of foreign exchange reserves and these reserves grow by over a $1 billion a day. At this rate, China will continue to have a major influence on foreign exchange markets, and foreign exchange and financial futures traders are well advised to follow their moves closely. Traditionally, the Chinese preferred to use their surpluses to buy safe, secure U.S. Treasury Bonds, but new liberalizing trends in the Chinese economy in addition to growing reserves from commercial success may mean changes in the types of investing they do. This new "sovereign wealth" has already led to new and different types of investing. Moving away from the tried and true government debt that was so long attractive to the Chinese, they are now becoming major influences in the private debt market. For example, in early 2007, the Chinese government invested $3 billion of its foreign exchange reserves in a private equity venture with

Blackstone, a New York based private equity firm. Some feel that the Chinese government may allocate as much as $300 billion of its assets for investment purposes. Other countries have sovereign wealth funds, such as South Korea's $20 billion and the United Arab Republic's $875 billion. Such funds have traditionally invested in very liquid assets such as precious metals or dollars, but signs are they may be following the example of China. In January of 2008, most of the $21 billion cash injected into Citibank and Merrill Lynch to rescue them from the subprime loan credit crisis was supplied by the governments of Singapore, Kuwait and South Korea. Perhaps the markets should expect more of these kinds of shifts to other different types of assets; any shift of this nature and magnitude will have a major impact on the forex market.

These are examples of some of the influences on the foreign exchange market. In addition to the fundamental factors, foreign exchange traders rely heavily on technical indicators and attempt to locate and follow trends using the tools that are more thoroughly discussed in Chapter Six.

STOCK INDEX FUTURES

Trading in listed equity options began in 1973 at the Chicago Board Options Exchange, the securities offshoot of the Chicago Board of Trade. In February, 1982, the Kansas City Board of Trade launched the first stock index futures contract on the Value Line. The Chicago Mercantile Exchange followed a few months later with its own S&P 500 Index contract. This contract became the market leader and today it is still the dominant U.S. stock index futures contract traded. The number of stock index futures and options contracts has grown and now traders speculative and hedging devices available to them in every area of market trading. Some of these contracts have been less successful than others, but the exchanges continue to develop innovative new instruments to offer traders. The most popular major index futures contracts are listed below.

Standard & Poor's 500 Index is by far the most popular of the stock index futures. It is a value-weighted index of 500 large-capitalization stocks traded on the New York Stock Exchange, the American Stock Exchange and the Nasdaq National Market System. The S&P 500 Index is capitalization-weighted, so those stocks with the most shares outstanding at the highest prices have the most influence on the index movement. The Standard & Poors 500 index, the basis for the futures index, was introduced in 1957, and is still the investment industry's standard for measuring portfolio performance.

When the Chicago Mercantile Exchange originally introduced S&P 500 futures in 1982, they traded at 500 times the cash index. As this market grew and became more and more popular, during the 1990s, the initial margin was viewed as too expensive for most traders. In response to market pressures, and to expand the participation in this contract, the CME decided to cut the contract's value to $250 times the index. In addition, the CME took an even further step to attract individual investors and offer risk management opportunities at an affordable price.

In 1997, they launched a smaller version of the popular S&P 500 futures contract, which they hoped would be more attractively sized for individual traders. Thus was born the E-mini S&P 500 futures contract, priced at one-fifth the size of the big contract at $50 times the index, and requiring a lower initial margin. Some say, however, that the real innovation and the strongest attraction of these new "mini" futures was that they traded on an electronic platform, and not in the traditional open-outcry pits. CME officials took a bold step that would place trading in these futures entirely on a trade-matching computer, which gave traders direct access to the market instead of having to trade through an order-handler. Prior to this decision, electronic trading was used only for after-hours trading or as a supplement to the primary pit contract; for the E-mini contracts, electronic trading would be the main market. Now that trading was going to be completely computer-based, the market could be kept open almost 24 hours a day. In only one year, the E-mini S&P futures became the third most active stock index contract in the country. Today, it has the largest volume of any U.S. stock index product. Even though it originated mainly as a product to attract small investors and speculators, because of its strong liquidity, it is now a favorite hedging vehicle for institutional investors as well.

The Nasdaq-100 Index is a modified market-capitalization index that includes the top 100 non-financial stocks listed on the Nasdaq Stock Market, including both domestic and foreign stocks. Because actively traded stocks such as Microsoft, Intel, eBay, Dell, Cisco, and many other computer related companies dominate the index, it is has come to be associated with the technology sector of the stock market.

Futures on the Nasdaq-100 began trading in 1996, and the initial value was $100 times the index. As happened with the S&P 500 Index, the value of the Nasdaq-100 rose dramatically during the 1990s, and therefore to attract a broader participation, the CME launched a mini-sized electronic contract. E-mini Nasdaq-100 futures are priced at only $20 times the index.

The E-mini S&P 500 futures and the E-mini Nasdaq-100 futures were over whelming successes. In fact, volume grew so quickly in both of these contracts that they overtook the larger futures benchmarks and opened the way for many other mini-sized futures products at the CME and other exchanges.

Dow Jones Industrial Average, commonly referred to as "the Dow" is an index of 30 large capitalization "blue chip" stocks traded on the New York Stock Exchange. Because of the equities it measures, it accounts for about 20 % of the total market value of all U.S. stocks. The Dow Jones Index was first published in 1896 and it is the most widely quoted market indicator throughout the world, consistently quoted in newspapers, radio, television and electronic media. It doesn't take a trader, or even a businessman to know that when someone in the media reports that the "stock market fell 20 points", the announcer is referring to the value of the thirty stocks that are listed on the Dow Jones Industrial Average. Futures on this important average began trading at the Chicago Board of Trade in 1997, but this only came about after fierce competition between all of the Chicago exchanges for the rights to trade futures and options on products owned by Dow Jones & Co. The Dow Jones trademark is an old and valued one, and Dow Jones was, at first, reluctant to allow its name to be used in trading.

The standard DJIA futures contract has a value of $10 times the average. The CBOT, following the trend for contracts that could appeal to a greater audience, began trading electronic, mini-sized DJIA futures valued at $5 times the average in 2002, and as occurred with the E-mini S&P contract, the mini-sized DJIA has become the more popular of the two with larger overall volume.

Single Stock Futures began trading in 2002 after many years of debate among regulators. The Johnson-Shad Accord of the early 1980s was the legislation that set the rules for stock index futures, but the Accord did not allow trading in futures on individual stocks and narrow-based stock indexes. These continued to be banned and did not become a trading opportunity until Congress passed the Commodity Futures Modernization Act of 2000.

This modernizing legislation allowed single-stock futures trading, and led to the creation of two new exchanges in November 2002. One of the two was a Chicago Limited Liability Corporation, OneChicago and was formed through a joint venture of the Chicago Mercantile Exchange, Chicago Board of Trade and Chicago Board Options Exchange; the other, NQLX, LLC was formed via a joint venture of Nasdaq and Euronext.liffe. (Currently, only OneChicago offers trading in the products; NQLX lost Nasdaq as a partner and then decided to suspend trading in December 2004 due to lack of interest.)

Single stock futures trade solely on an electronic platform in the United States, and each futures contract represents 100 shares of the underlying stock. Despite their initial controversy as well as all of the effort that was devoted to development, single-stock futures have not caught on in the market as had been hoped and expected.

VOLATILITY FUTURES

Volatility is an important factor in pricing options: high volatility usually signals expensive options premiums, low volatility means lower options premiums. Volatility index (Vix) futures were introduced to address this added risk in trading options. VIX futures are based on the Volatility Index, a concept first introduced in 1993 in a paper in the Journal of Derivatives by Professor Robert E. Whaley of Duke University. It is a measure of market expectations of near term volatility conveyed by the S&P 500 stock index options prices. Trading in VIX futures was launched in March, 2004 by CBOE Futures Exchange, LLC. The CBOE intended this index to become an indicator of stock market "sentiment" among investors and introduced it in order to "reflect investors' consensus view of expected stock market volatility over the next 30 days."

The next effort to address these kinds of risk was the "realized variance" futures contract. In May 2004, the CBOE CFE launched the CBOE S&P 500 three month variance futures contract. This is an exchange-traded futures contract based on the realized variance of the Standard & Poor's 500 stock Index over a three-month period.

Traders, hedgers and speculators look to innovations in these derivatives markets to protect their positions or to take advantage of spreads between buy and sell prices. One set of parties (traders and hedgers) is willing to pay the other (speculators) to reduce some of the risk of holding their position in foreign exchange, stocks and options.

CASE STUDY: TK TRADING

What are the qualities you need to successfully trade commodities?

Discipline, patience and risk tolerance.

Which commodities do you prefer to trade and why?

I prefer to trade the grains and crude oil because usually the options are fairly priced and there is always something moving those markets.

Are there certain markets you won't trade in?

I won't trade illiquid markets such as lumber.

What is your favorite (or has been most successful) strategy?

I mostly trade long options, calls and puts.

What's the hardest thing to do or decision to make in trading?

The hardest decision is to cut losses because many people attach their egos to their trades.

Do you rely on fundamentals or technical analysis more?

I believe in using fundamental analysis to decide what I think the long term trend will be and then I use the technicals for entry and exit points.

Which technical indicator do you rely on the most?

I use a very basic trend line to decide whether to buy sell or hold a certain position.

Do you trade full time or part time?

Can a part time trader have real success? I trade full time and I think a part time trader can be successful if they have strict entry and exit points as soon as they enter the trade.

CASE STUDY: TK TRADING

What are your best knowledge resources?

The internet has so much free information that just about anyone can know what the professionals know.

What was your most successful trade?

I have had option premiums quintuple in the time span of about one week.

Least successful?

I have had lots of options expire over the years but the worst story that I ever heard about was an investor who invested $20,000 in lumber futures and got caught in over a week's worth of limit moves against him. In the end he lost over $200,000.

What do you think right now about:

Oil – Long term bull

Wheat- The top is in.

Corn- Long term bull

Beans- Long term bull

Coffee- Short term bull

Gold- Long term bull

Dollar- Long term bear

What's the most interesting/funny/strange story you have that is related to commodities trading?

I love to hear the stories where an investor makes a killing in a market like soybeans and uses the money to buy a bass boat or take a trip around the world.

14

A FINAL WORD FROM THE EXPERTS

As we have observed here, trading actual futures contracts is a complicated business, even though the forces that affect the prices of so-called "soft" agricultural and livestock commodities can be simpler to understand than the complex economic factors that influence stock or bond prices and financial futures. In commodities, it all boils down to supply, which is largely determined by weather and demand. Futures markets are an important harbinger of important economic trends: the first signs of inflation, the direction of consumer preferences, and the changing cost of feeding and nourishing an average family are frequently reflected first in the prices of our basic raw materials. Commodity prices are quick to respond to economic shocks such as decreased supply, whether due to natural causes such as weather related shortages, or to political causes such as manipulations by OPEC in the oil supply. This is because of the highly liquid and competitive environment of trading in commodities-commodities prices react instantaneously to events, or even the interpretation of events. Not so the prices of finished products, which are fixed at the factory, by the middle man and then at the retail level. The closer a product is to its raw state, the more quickly its price will adjust to reflect changing economic basics.

For investors, there is another important reason to keep a close eye on commodity prices. Even if an investor is not interested in cornering the market on soybeans or silver, most of the world's largest companies (and their share prices) are significantly impacted by changing commodity prices.

Profit margins at the Swiss food giant Nestlé, for example, will depend partly on the price of cocoa. McDonald's and other fast-food chains have a huge interest in the price of cattle and pork bellies. Most food companies buy literally tons of sugar. Experts say, moreover, that a number of commodities will undergo dramatic price swings in the near future. Any investor following the fortunes of these companies would be lax if he did not consider the impact their raw materials prices would have on the performance of their stocks.

Following is a sampling of professional opinion on the commodity markets that are expected to make strong moves up or down in the year ahead.

ENERGY

Who better to look to for predictions in the energy field than the biggest player of all, ExxonMobile? In their Outlook for Energy: A View to 2030, they contend that world progress, including population growth and improved living standards, will drive the demand for more and more energy, up to 60% more by 2030, compared to 2000. Most of the world's growing use of energy will be met by oil, gas and coal, but they also project that as energy needs increase the world will become more efficient in energy use, and alternate sources will be exploited more. As the report so pithily puts it, "We are a world on the move and liquid fuels are essential to meet these demands."

But where is the increased efficiency, and what is the status of the alternate sources? Increased demand will fuel increased prices in the short run- that is the basic premise of the supply/demand model of price theory. The corollary is that supply should increase in order to trap these attractive higher prices. In the case of non renewable goods such as certain commodities (oil, precious metals, etc.), however, the supply cannot increase, or cannot increase substantially. Since supply chases demand, if a supply cannot be increased, logic would dictate that new supplies or new goods will be substituted. If this is the case, why hasn't more progress been made in the pursuit of alternative fuel sources, such as biofuels, solar or wind energy? New sources are being developed but not at the pace that would be expected in the face of what is increasingly being considered a worldwide crisis in energy demand. Alternate sources are certainly talked about a great deal, but despite all the hype, each year sees the world more dependent upon petroleum products while alternative fuel sources are marginal in comparison. What does this spell for the energy markets? Why have not alternate energy sources overtaken the carbon fuel market?

One of the problems is the cost of alternatives. Some critics have claimed that ethanol has a negative "net energy balance"; in other words, it requires more energy to produce than it yields in fuel. (Net energy is the amount of energy in a fuel minus the amount of energy it takes to produce it.) If corn and soybean prices continue to escalate based on the perceived demand for ethanol, this negative balance will only increase. A study by Simla Tokgoz of the Center for Agriculture and Rural Development of Iowa State University forecasts that a projected increase in ethanol production from a present level of 5 trillion gallons to 14 trillion gallons in 2016 would translate to a 44 % increase in the price of corn and a 22% increase in the price of soybeans. This is in view of the strong competition for the use of these grains in other markets, such as animal feed and human consumption. Given these pressures, the costs of biofuel production will not become competitive with petroleum fuels unless other major changes (new carbon fuel discoveries/more efficient use of fuel/new methods of producing or processing biofuels) become part of our new reality.

Another alternative that has been discussed is biodiesel fuels. Biodiesel fuels are produced from animal fats or used vegetable oils. Biodiesel actually performs better than the petroleum diesel that is extensively used today, but currently the cost of production is about three times as much as the cost of petroleum diesel. This is according to Biodiesel Online, a site that advocates the use, or at least the study of the feasibility of the use of this fuel. To this weakness, add the argument of many that biofuels in general produce more greenhouse gases than oil and gasoline. According to a report in the Times (U.K.) in September of 2007:

"Rapeseed and maize biodiesels were calculated to produce up to 70 per cent and 50 per cent more greenhouse gases respectively than fossil fuels. The concerns were raised over the levels of emissions of nitrous oxide, which is 296 times more powerful as a greenhouse gas than carbon dioxide. Scientists found that the use of biofuels released twice as much as nitrous oxide as previously realized. The research team found that 3 to 5 per cent of the nitrogen in fertiliser was converted and emitted. In contrast, the figure used by the International Panel on Climate Change, which assesses the extent and impact of man-made global warming, was 2 per cent. The findings illustrated the importance, the researchers said, of ensuring that measures designed to reduce greenhouse-gas emissions are assessed thoroughly before being hailed as a solution."

The true picture of alternative fuel sources such as biofuels and biodiesels is still unclear in the minds of many traders. Political pressures to assuage the conservationists and the farm lobby have led to massive subsidies that may artificially protect the true cost of biofuels. In the opposite camp are those (led by oil companies) who focus on the weaknesses of these alternatives. The fact may simply be that alternative fuels are a long way from being substitutes for petroleum products.

If ethanol and biodiesel are still years or decades away from being cost effective petroleum substitutes, logic would suggest that new sources of petroleum products would be explored. The issue here is that other sources of petroleum are either more expensive to tap, or are located in politically risky areas of the world.

Christophe de Margerie, the CEO of Total, the French oil giant, predicted in 2007 that the world would never be able to increase the output of oil from the current 85 million barrels per day to the predicted 2030 requirement of 120 million barrels per day from the present supply sources. He, like many others, believes that the oil necessary to meet future demand must come from areas that are not currently being tapped. This is not so simple. Newer oil fields are in difficult areas for extraction, such as deeper waters, or fields that contain much more solid oil, not as easily extractable as the oil in the oil rich deserts of the Gulf region. The capital required to exploit these regions is not easy to raise, not, at least, at today's oil prices. Here is a true price spiral conundrum: oil prices have to increase dramatically for it to be worthwhile for investors to expand operations in more difficult areas. Since the idea of increasing supply is to bring down prices, the purpose is lost. And in areas where this liquid gold is easier to extract, such as Venezuela and Iran, the governments may not be as cooperative about supplying it to western world guzzlers.

METALS

Metalminer, a site dedicated to "sourcing and trading intelligence for the global metals market" gives us the following predictions for metals:

- Reduced demand and lower raw material prices, especially nickel, will result in lower steel prices.

- Rising energy prices and reduction in supply due to the closing of aging plants will cause aluminum prices to remain high.

- Copper and zinc will continue to be in high demand, but new capacity is being developed, and therefore price pressures will not be as strong. These are very volatile markets, however, since non trade speculators are active in them.

- In general, slowing growth in the United States and western Europe should be offset by demand from growth in the Asian economies, so do not expect any substantial price erosion due to recessionary economies.

FOODS

Clearly, predicting future commodities price levels is important to major producers and traders. The global grain marketing company, Bunge, Inc. has even developed a system whereby it rewards local farmers who share their predictions about crop plantings, yields, etc. In their weekly "Farmetrics" game, players compete to accurately predict important agricultural statistics in order to win trips or farm equipment. Bunge uses this information to help with important marketing and business decisions, believing that the farmer in the field may be one of the best experts on the subject.

Here are some predictions from Fiona Boal, executive director of food and agribusiness research and Michael Whitehead, analyst, for Rabobank in its food and agricultural outlook report:

- Corn and ethanol production will double by 2015.

- The current level of 300 million gallons of biodiesel will increase by 50% over the next two years.

- Wheat acreage will increase, but anxiety about

current supplies will mean that any negative news will push prices upwards.

- Competing use for grains and oilseeds (for fuel) will mean price inflation for livestock feed.

Those who believe caffeine makes their hearts race should avoid coffee futures, according to many market observers. When frosts hit Brazil's crops, estimates for total production can be reduced by as much as half. This extreme dependence upon weather factors, primarily because of the limitations on where coffee can be grown, makes for a very volatile market. In its November 2006 coffee report, the International Coffee Organization (ICO) estimated a world production deficit in 2007-2008 of at least 6.6 million bags. For calendar year 2007, the ICO estimated consumption at 117 million bags, up from 116 million bags in 2006.The official 2007-08 forecast estimates a crop size of between 31.1 and 32.3 million bags. This indicates a return to a world deficit of supply related to demand and continued downward pressure on stocks with upward pressure on prices. This deficit is likely to be at least as large as that in 2005-06 in spite of more favorable economic conditions for production in other exporting countries. Clearly they predict a shortage of coffee and although Vietnam is now a significant producer the quality is poor. Technically the market is in an early phase of a bullish move, according to CTG Futures.

GRAINS

In what they call the "biofuels bonanza", the Directorate-General for Agriculture and Rural Development of the

European Commission, citing the surge in commodity prices, thinks that it seems reasonable to ask if biofuels have somehow changed the fundamentals of world agricultural markets. In their 2007 Outlook for World Agricultural Commodity Markets, they predict that the overall outlook is for continued high prices, as anticipated by both the Food and Agricultural Policy Research Institute (FAPRI) and the OECD-FAO already last year. According to this report, FAPRI expects corn and vegetable oils to be up by some 50%, wheat and dairy products up 40%, oilseeds and sugar by 20-26% and meat prices by 12-14% compared to the average of the past decade. Oilmeals, however, are forecast to be down by 4%. Over the next few years, the U.S. Department of Agriculture also predicts that a rapid increase in global production of biofuels will change the traditional price relationship among some of the major commodities. Despite the many negatives involved in the production of ethanol, increased demand for corn for ethanol in the United States has pushed up corn prices relative to other grains and soybeans. Today, the world's farmlands are being relied on for both food and fuel, and these competing uses for grains and oilseeds will also put upward pressure prices on livestock feed prices.

LIVESTOCK

According to Darrell Mark, University of Nebraska-Lincoln livestock marketing specialist, profits are to be had in the livestock. Feed cattle prices have been at record highs on average in 2007, and prices in 2008 could be just as high, he said. As with crops, increasing input costs will be a challenge, with corn prices, in particular, being driven higher by ethanol demand. According to Mark, "Feed prices will continue to be high, but more importantly, will be volatile".

On the hog side, prices are likely to be 2 percent to 3 percent lower than in 2007 as pork production is forecast to increase, Mark said. Rising feed costs will also be a factor.

Because of record production, U.S. hog farmers have suffered large losses recently. In addition, health-conscious consumers have switched from fatty bacon to leaner cuts of meat. That, analysts say, has had a serious impact on commodity prices. Pork bellies, for example, were trading at a discount to whole hog prices over the past few years. But lately, a trend among fast-food restaurants to offer sandwiches that include bacon has given pork belly prices a lift.

15

MOVING FORWARD

What are the future trends in commodities?
Will new commodities start to be traded?

Goldman Sachs tells us that commodity funds have $100 billion to invest in the commodity markets in 2007. China has $1 trillion in cash reserves that are primarily in U.S. dollars that it will have to invest and it has expressed an interest in diversifying its investment mix in 2007. Perhaps a large portion of these reserves will end up in going into commodities. How will such an infusion of investment funds affect the commodities and financial futures markets?

New products, new technologies, and emerging markets mean there will always be change in the commodity markets. We do know is that change is inevitable and understanding and being able to adjust to changes is probably the key to financial success, whatever the market.

Remember that we said gold was trading for about $100 an ounce in August 1976. Less than four years later, in January 1980, it peaked at $875—an 875 percent increase in three and a half years, approximately a 250% annual rate of return. This is only the increase due to the actual price changes; trading on margin would have yielded an outrageous profit potential. How many traders could predict a move of this magnitude and then have the stamina to ride this wave to its peak? Then, of course, the trader had to get out at the right time. At the $875 peak, there were predictions of $1,000–$2,000 per ounce price per gold. (As it happens, the January 1980 high remains the all-time high price.)

If you were convinced the bull run in gold would continue in 1979 and bought gold at $220 early in the year, a record high at the time, how would you have reacted to the market? The market moved in an orderly pattern until it hit $441 in early October. Then it started heading lower. What do you think you would have done when the market began its decline, which, of course at this point you do not know is a decline, but may only be a short-term correction. You have doubled your money by trading in gold in less than a year, a 100% move, and many times this gain if you worked on margin. You are faced with a frenzied market and it starts to drop, first 5%, then 10%. Would you have taken your profit at this point? After 10%? The falling gold market went below $370 in early November, a 17% correction. Some one would have to have been a pretty committed bull not to cash out at this time. But these massive moves will appear tame compared to what was to come. Gold, which had doubled from $220 to $440 in only 10 months, doubled again in just another three months. In retrospect, the October-to-November 17% decline looks like a minor correction on the charts. It appears to be a flag formation (see Chapter Six, Technical Trading). Once the flag was broken to the upside (in November), all hell broke loose and gold soared to its 1980 all-time high of $875. Could this happen again? Would you as a trader be able to ride this wave to take advantage of this volatile market? We can't predict the future, but if we apply the movements from the past to the present situation, another doubling would put gold at $1,450.

One of the limitations of examining these performance results is that they have the benefit of hindsight. Hypothetical trading does not involve financial risk, and no hypothetical trading record can take into account for the impact of risking one's one money in actual trading. The ability to withstand losses and continue to adhere to a particular trading philosophy despite trading losses can affect actual trading results. A trader thinks very differently when there is an actual margin call and he has to come up with the money.

The commodity markets have seen excellent performance over recent years, but in relative terms are still rather inexpensive right now. Oil prices are an exception, of course, but from 1990 to 2007, the price of gold has increased 67% from about $410 an ounce to about $684 (falling off its record high in May 2006 of $730 an ounce). In contrast, the DJIA during the same period increased from about 2,625 to 13,264, a five-fold increase, and with the housing price boom of recent years, the median home price in the United States has grown from $90,000 to $240,000, according to USA Today. Perceived intelligence would suggest that these other assets must flatten out or decline in price (as has already happened in real estate), while commodities continue to grow. The prior bear market in commodities has reduced capacity while worldwide demand is on the increase. (See the expert's opinions, below.)

Understanding why these increases occur is the key. Someone who entered the gold market in the spring of 2006 would not agree that gold has shown sustained increases in value over the years. Even the most bullish commodities trader recognizes the cyclical nature of commodities and there is no financial asset class that trades in a straight line—there are always ups and downs. But there are major trends that a savvy investor can use to his advantage, and there are also ways of spotting short-term hiccups in a market that can be capitalized upon to take profits along the way.

Recent turbulent weather patterns have affected the commodities markets with a double whammy: reduced production coupled with the desire for stockpiling in case of continued weather-related turbulence. An example of this is the sugar market. The devastating hurricanes, storms, and tornadoes has affected sugar crops, and increased demand for sugar as an ingredient in ethanol has put further pressure on prices. Weather-related problems also affect markets other than agricultural products, such as oil, when refineries are shut down, or lumber, when new construction becomes necessary. Many feel that unsettled weather patterns are with us for good, a result of global change, so why not be the one to take advantage of the forces of nature?

Many factors point to a long term commodities bull market. Here is a brief synopsis of some of the expert's opinions:

"The current supply-and-demand balance for commodities worldwide is way out of whack-a classic sign of a long bull market on the way."

—Jim Rogers, Hot Commodities

"The 21st century is going to experience the largest population growth in the history of humankind.....Put simply, significant population growth translates into greater global demand for commodities. Humans are the most voracious consumers of raw materials on the planet – and the only ones who pay for them. As the number of humans in the world increases, so will the demand for natural resources."

—Amine Bouchentouf, *Commodities for Dummies*

"The world is scrambling for resources-to power our cars, to heat and cool our houses, to keep technology speeding along. At best, these resources are finite; at worst, they're well on their way to disappearing altogether. That's why now is the perfect time to jump into these markets and profit from these trends."

—Kevin Kerr, *A Maniac Commodity Trader's Guide to Making a Fortune*

"There are three major reasons for the current rush into commodities. The first is that world economic, financial and political trends and conditions have

*turned hostile since 2000, and consequently
stocks and bonds have not done so well over the
past five or six years. ... Second, a recent round
of academic and market research has shown that
commodities can stand up as equals to stocks and
bonds as investments. ... The third reason is that
commodities prices have been rising, and investors
chase rising prices."*

—Jeffrey M. Christian, Commodities Rising

The underlying theme among all of these experts is that commodities, the raw materials of our lives, are in relatively inelastic supply and the pressures of population growth and worldwide economic expansion weigh on that supply, forcing prices up over the long term. In other words, it's all about supply and demand.

As Bouchentouf points out, we may be at the beginning of the largest population growth in history. This is in terms of real population numbers. Add to this the phenomenon of entire societies economically liberated over the past decade. The world will face increased demand for commodities even without increased population. Historically, this kind of growth has impelled enormous riches: witness the success of the oil barons during the industrial revolution. Today, commodity-based wealth continues to grow. But it must be noted that not all commodities go up all the time. There are complex issues involved.

DEVELOPING A FUTURE TRADING PHILOSOPHY

There have always been losers in the commodities markets, even when commodities prices were on a strong uptrend. How does a trader ensure that he will be one of the winners?

When in doubt, stay out. Many factors may be at work in undermining your confidence in a certain trade. If your instinct gives you doubts, you are much better off not entering the market. If you have done enough study and research, this "second sense" will serve you well in your trading decisions.

Limit losses and let profits accumulate. This cannot be emphasized enough. Set up your trading program so that stops are entered to limit your potential losses. Be bold enough to get out of a position that is not performing as your analysis said it should. But if you have a good trend running, stick with it and don't get cold feet. Your can also limit your losses by setting a maximum dollar per trade approach to trading. Stay away from pyramiding—let your profits accumulate rather than increase the number of contracts.

Do not overtrade. Execution costs can be very expensive if you trade small positions and you trade them too frequently. You will lose track of your trading plan if you are constantly switching from one trade to another.

Do not be afraid to sell short. Most non-hedgers are wary of selling short, which should make it all the more attractive to speculators. If you have determined that a commodity is poised for a fall in price, you have two choices: stand aside (remember, that is also a position) or go short.

Only invest when potential profit is several times the potential loss. This is one of the most important rules to follow. Don't bet the farm when all you can make is a small profit in return. With proper analysis, you can determine your potential profits vs. your potential losses.

Trade with the trend, not against it. It is believed in the commodities trading markets, that the tried and true maxim "the trend is your friend" cannot be overstated. Patterns are the best indicators of market behavior.

Never meet a margin call; liquidate instead. This is the easiest, if most drastic way, to limit your losses. The market is telling you that you are in a losing position. Listen to the market.

Get information on the current economic situation and commodity markets, keep on top if it, and make sure your understand it. Take advice, but do your own research to confirm it. Even if you receive valuable information, devote the time necessary to confirm how it will impact your trading position. In order to find out all you can about commodities, keep an inquiring mind; if you don't understand the answer to something that puzzles you, keep digging until it makes sense.

More emotion equals less profit. Remain cool, calm, and collected at all times. It will be a lot easier to do this if you have planned your trades properly, accepted the possibility of losses (that you will limit through stops, options, or not meeting margin calls) and stick to your plan.

Be well capitalized. Do not trade with such a small amount that you lose before you really get started. If you can't afford to lose the capital, you should not be in the market in the first place.

Develop a plan that will build a strong foundation in trading and will help you realize the most profit with the least risk. (Remember that there may not always be a profit, but there will always be a risk.)

Do not trade in any market you do not know or understand. If you have been trading one commodity for a while and want to expand your horizons, start all over again and learn everything you can about it. New commodities are traded from time to time as well, and "getting in on the bottom" may have its value in the stock market, but relatively new, untested markets are probably not the place for a new trader to be hanging out.

Respect the concept of margins. Realize that it is a tool that can be of great advantage when you use the leveraging concept properly, but that is can also drastically increase your exposure to loss if you are not careful.

Expect, and be prepared, for setbacks. Even if we are in a strong bull market for commodities, corrections will occur and prices will go down. (That may be a signal to buy more!) But discipline and sticking to one's trading philosophy allows for some ups and downs along the way.

It requires discipline and courage, and there are many trading opportunities out there, but be careful. As Richard Waldron warns us in Futures 101: "Investing in the futures industry has huge potential for earning profits for any trader. ... Just don't jump into it until you understand the language, financial pitfalls and potential losses." It is up to you. Louis Pasteur, famed biologist, must have known something about it when he observed that: "Chance favors the informed mind."

BIBLIOGRAPHY

Rogers, Jim, *Hot Commodities How Anyone Can Invest Profitable in the World's Best Market*, Random House, 2007

Kerr, Kevin, A *Maniac Commodity Trader's Guide to Making A Fortune*, John Wiley & Sons, 2007

Christian, Jeffrey M., *Commodities Rising*, John Wiley & Sons, 2007

Barrie, Scott W., *Commodity Trader's Almanac*, John Wiley & Sons, 2007

Bouchentouf, Amine, *Commodities for Dummies*, Wiley Publishing, Inc., 2007

Murphy, John, *Technical Analysis of the Futures Market*, Prentiss Hall, 1999

Kleinman, George, T*rading Commodities and Financial Futures*, Pearson Education, 2005

Kennedy, Paul, *Preparing for the Twenty-First Century*, First Vintage Books, 1994

Waldron, Richard, *Futures 101, An Introductory to Commodity Trading*, Squantum Publishing, 2003

Bollinger, *John, Bollinger on Bollinger Bands*, **www. bollingerbands.com**

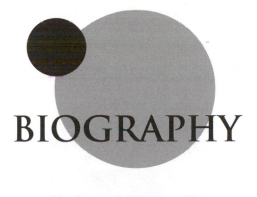

BIOGRAPHY

After thirty years in the corporate world of Financial Management, twenty of which were spent at a commodities trading firm, Mary Holihan decided to capitalize on this valuable business experience by embarking on a career in writing on business related topics.

INDEX